Big Business and Free Men

Big Business

————————— A N D

Free Men

by James C. Worthy

FOREWORD BY
F. B. McCONNELL

HARPER & BROTHERS, PUBLISHERS
New York

MY 23 '60 Barrett 2.80

Foreword

BY F. B. McCONNELL,
Chairman of the Board Sears, Roebuck and Co.

This is a book about basic issues: the place of business in modern society; the consequences of the rise of large-scale economic organization; the emerging leadership role of the businessman. It seeks to demonstrate—to my mind effectively—that big business and human values are not mutually exclusive but complementary. This theme is inherent in the title, *Big Business* AND *Free Men.*

This is not a "defense" of business. Rather, it is a searching analysis of some of the strengths and weaknesses of modern business management, and an effort to point management thinking along constructive and creative lines.

No one could have written this book without intimate, personal experience as a member of a large business organization. Mr. Worthy has been with Sears, Roebuck and Co. for more than twenty years, and has worked his way up in a tough competitive environment to his present position as vice president in charge of public relations. In addition, he has been active in political, governmental, and civic affairs. He has not only had a wealth of experience with organizations of many kinds, but has sought to think critically and objectively about that experience.

While Mr. Worthy writes from a standpoint of proved and tested knowledge, he writes as a private citizen and not as a spokesman for Sears, Roebuck and Co. This is as it should be, for he is first of all a citizen and only secondarily an officer of a corporation.

The reader may not agree with all of Mr. Worthy's conclusions, but no one with any experience in business (or with business) can disagree about the importance of the issues raised. Those who may disagree must take the responsibility of thinking their way through to conclusions of their own.

This book should command the serious attention of responsible citizens in all walks of life.

Preface

This is a book written *by* a businessman, primarily *for* businessmen—although an author's pride leads him to hope that it will find an audience among people in all walks of life concerned with some of the basic problems of American industrial society.

This is a book *about* the businessman, especially the big businessman. It makes no pretenses to scholarly research; rather, it grows out of concrete experience in the world of business, and represents an effort to evaluate that experience in terms of traditional American values.

Much has been written about big business as an economic institution, but little is known of it as a human and social institution. This book seeks, in some measure, to fill that void.

Primarily, however, the book seeks to explore the role of business in modern American life, the means for preserving the essentials of human freedom within the structure of large-scale organization, and the emerging responsibilities of business within a democratic social order.

If I am sometimes critical of business, it is only because I am anxious to correct those shortcomings which are most directly within the power of businessmen to correct. If I appear to gloss over some of the problems posed by the emergence of a powerful labor movement, it is not because I consider them unimportant but because I am chiefly concerned with the role and responsibilities of the businessman rather than with those of the labor leader or the legislator.

The opinions expressed are my own and do not necessarily reflect the policies of my company. Many of my colleagues will not be in full agreement with all I have said, and on some points they will be in strong disagreement. I suggest that this fact in itself is evidence of a certain spirit of freedom within the modern corporation and that the pressures for conformity are not as great as they are sometimes thought to be.

I am deeply indebted to Mrs. Robert Popper for her editorial assistance in the preparation of the manuscript; to Mr. Peter F. Drucker for his help in thinking through some of the problems of exposition; to Mr. Ordway Tead for his critical advice as publisher; to Mr. Theodore V. Houser and the Honorable Sinclair Weeks for reading the manuscript in its entirety and for giving me a number of helpful suggestions; to Miss Helen Grove and Mr. Dean Webbles for assistance in final editing; and to Miss Grace Wells for typing the successive versions of the manuscript during its course of composition.

Above all, I am indebted to my wife for her patience, understanding, and encouragement during the trying period when this book was struggling to see the light of day.

James C. Worthy

Winnetka, Illinois
April, 1959

Contents

PART I

The Public Posture of Business

PART II

The Political Economy of Industrial Organization

PART III

Business Citizenship and American Democracy

Part ONE

The Public Posture of Business

The Self-conscious Businessman

I

Business in America occupies a place of unique prestige and power. Collectively, businessmen represent one of the leadership groups of our society. Here there is no landed gentry, ancient nobility, or party elite to compete with, and high social position itself is usually based on means and status acquired in business pursuits. Businessmen enjoy wealth above average levels and with it the respect accorded wealth. They have a remarkable record of philanthropy, both as individual and as corporate donors, and they benefit from the prestige which philanthropy confers. Their control of economic resources vests them with great power, in the use of which they are permitted wide discretion.

Nor is their power confined to economic affairs. They are consulted on all matters involving the welfare of the community, and their advice carries weight. Businessmen sit on the boards of universities, are active in church affairs, and provide leadership in a broad variety of civic causes. They are appointed, and sometimes elected, to important government

posts. Under the New Deal they exercised a considerable
influence on government affairs, however antagonistic many
of them were to what they felt the New Deal represented;
under the Eisenhower administration their influence is still
more marked. They are recipients of many honors from an
admiring citizenry.

The business system itself is one of the key institutions of
American society. Business occupies in the American scheme
of things a place it occupies nowhere else in the world. The
position of business in the American institutional framework
is one of major significance.

Nevertheless, businessmen tend to feel uneasy about their
position. Large numbers of people seem to look on the business
system with skepticism, suspicion, and hostility. Powerful
groups are thought to be unfriendly to business and committed to its subversion. In many business circles the threat of
subversion is considered a real and present danger; in fact,
the process of subversion is sometimes conceived as already far
advanced toward the dissolution of the business system as we
know it. Businessmen often display strong feelings of de-
fensiveness, suspicion of the motives of others, and pessimism
about the future of business and of the country.

Nor are these apprehensions difficult to account for. From
1932 until 1952, American voters returned to office national
administrations which the great majority of businessmen be-
lieved were antagonistic to business—and the campaign ora-
tory of the successful Presidential candidates did little to allay
their anxiety. It was only natural for businessmen to assume
that many people in this country—at least a majority large
enough to elect Presidents—were "anti-business."

A considerable amount of legislation during the thirties was
enacted on the basis of anti-business slogans, an effective
means at the time for securing passage of legislation whose
success might otherwise have been doubtful. However much

business suffered in fact under the New Deal and Fair Deal,
there can be no doubt that the psychic damage was severe. The
labels attached to many important enactments created a strong
sense of insecurity in the business community. Just as labor
opposition to the Taft-Hartley Act was largely based on the
fact that it was conceived and promoted as an "anti-union"
measure, so "anti-business" legislation created similar anxieties
and resentment among businessmen.

The rise of organized labor has been another source of
anxiety. The violent attacks on business in the course of organizing campaigns; contract demands encroaching on
"management prerogatives"; charges of "exorbitant profits,"
"unconscionable profiteering," "price gouging," and like
epithets give businessmen cause to fear the great power of
organized labor and to see in that power a challenge to their
own leadership and a threat to the integrity of the business
system.

The businessman is disturbed that other groups do not
always share his values. Large numbers of people have little
idea how the business system works, and there is widespread
misunderstanding about such subjects as profits, the relation
between investment and jobs, the relation of productivity to
living standards, and other matters which businessmen consider of prime importance. Tax policies are especially vex-
atious. Taxes affecting business seem to be levied with little
concern for the needs of healthy economic growth, and much
of the personal income of businessmen is conscripted by
steeply progressive income taxes.

The skepticism of "intellectuals" toward business is especially disturbing. Negative attitudes toward businessmen
and the business system are reflected in novels, plays, and the
visual arts. The businessman is typically portrayed in a manner which he can only regard as caricature. The treatment of
the role of business by economic historians is often widely at

variance with the businessman's concept of that role. Writers, artists, and scholars display a lamentable tendency—or so it often appears—to side with labor in controversial situations and to support public policies which businessmen oppose. The business community is sensitive to criticisms of its ethics by such bodies as the National Council of the Churches of Christ in America, and the wide vogue of the "social gospel" is a source of disquiet. Altogether, the businessman often feels that his values are not understood or appreciated in circles with significant public influence.

Representatives of big business feel particularly vulnerable. As *Time* magazine once observed, "Big business remains the shorthand for everything that is evil." Big business is enjoined by law and public opinion from certain types of action which are permitted and widely approved for other groups. If big business restricts output to increase prices it is guilty of "restraint of trade." Pursuit of the same ends by small business is applauded as "fair trade," by organized labor as "collective bargaining," and by farmers as "parity." The semantic differences are striking.

Thus for all the undoubted power and prestige of the businessman in contemporary society, he is frequently ill at ease.

II

That some businessmen have over-reacted to what they consider evidence of hostility is explainable in part by the circumstances in which they operate. The nature of experience within a hierarchy (in this case the business organization) tends to create an acute sensitivity to criticism. Organized activity requires a high degree of consensus, and evidence of lack of consensus is disturbing to those in positions of responsibility. Furthermore, ways of behavior within a hierarchy tend to enforce a certain amount of deference to those in authority, who come through force of habit and human frailty to expect such behavior, including agreement on controversial subjects, not only from their subordinates but from others as well.

Sensitivity to criticism and expectation of the acceptance of ideas encourage feelings that "those who are not with us must be against us." Such feelings are not peculiar to businessmen; they are typical of those who live and work within hierarchical organizations: government officials, labor leaders, educators, administrators of all varieties. It is not surprising that feelings of this kind are found in exaggerated form in that most hierarchical of all modern political and economic organizations, the Soviet Union.

Nevertheless, businessmen need to be more appreciative of the virtues of dissent and criticism, not only from the outside but from within their own organizations as well. They need to recognize the role of dissent in a free society, and they need to understand what would happen to such a society if any important institution within it should ever be effectively insulated from criticism. This applies as much to business as it does to government or labor—two institutions the criticism of which the businessman is not likely to forgo.

Criticism is an effective means for identifying and correcting mistakes before they become so serious that drastic measures are necessary, including measures imposed from without. Business itself has been one of the chief beneficiaries of this critical process. The late nineteenth century was rife with abuses that would not be tolerated today. In the perspective of history, the amazing thing is not that such conditions existed but that they were eliminated so quickly. Sometimes but by no means always corrective action came through legislation. Often business itself moved to remedy its own shortcomings, in response either to public pressure or to the businessman's own sense of the fitness of things. Abuses which seem extreme from the vantage point of the mid-twentieth century, and which must have appeared intractable at the time, were rectified, usually within the generation in which they emerged. The business system itself is stronger for that rectification.

This change would not have taken place if there had been any serious interference with the process of public criticism. Criticism is never pleasant for those who are criticized. But just as pain serves a vital purpose in protecting an organism, so criticism serves a vital purpose in preserving the integrity of an institution. While the businessman needs to be alert and even sensitive to criticism, he would do well to keep its values in mind as well.

III

Even with full acceptance of the virtues of dissent and criticism, the businessman is rightfully concerned with improving the environment of public opinion in which business operates and building stronger support for public policies that will foster and not impede the performance of its social function.

Businessmen have not been inactive on this score. There is seldom a meeting of a business association where the problem of public attitudes toward business does not occupy an important place on the agenda. For some years both the National Association of Manufacturers and the United States Chamber of Commerce have warned their members against complacency, urging them to be alert to the threats they are facing, and counseling them on the kind of action they ought to be taking to win more friends for business. Other business organizations are similarly active.

Plant-community relations programs have been developed by many companies, especially in the manufacturing field, to foster local good will and public support. Economic education programs for employees enjoy a wide vogue. Institutional advertising campaigns, typically extolling the virtues of "free enterprise" and the American way of life, are directed toward the public at large. The techniques employed for "reaching" all these groups run the full gamut of the public relations art: speeches, books and pamphlets, conferences, discussion groups, plant tours, newspaper and magazine advertising, radio and television, syndicated columns, house organs—even comic books.

There is reason to doubt, however, that these efforts have been particularly effective. By and large, people already favorably disposed toward business have responded favorably; those who were apathetic or disinterested (probably the majority) have responded with apathy; those who were hostile have remained hostile.

A major weakness of many such efforts is the naïve assumption that with knowledge will come acceptance. But economists who have spent lifetimes studying economic phenomena by no means see eye to eye. Nor has knowledge of economic "facts" eliminated conflicts among businessmen themselves, as witness the perennial controversies over taxation, tariffs, and other matters where different businessmen draw different conclusions from the same sets of circumstances. Knowledge of economic principles is not likely to be any more effective in eliminating conflicts between workers and employers or in fostering better understanding between business and the public.

Beyond this fundamental weakness, most programs of economic education suffer from two shortcomings: a tendency toward the oversimplification of ideas which are inherently complex, and a penchant for using techniques that have proved successful in selling merchandise but are poorly adapted to the purpose of gaining acceptance for ideas.

Oversimplification is probably the more serious. Economic processes are complex and a knowledge of how the business system operates cannot be inculcated by a few easy lessons. In the nature of things, business cannot afford the time or the payroll that would be needed to impart to its employees even the equivalent of an elementary introduction to economics. It has sought, therefore, to condense the content of its courses to a few "broad principles" and a few "basic facts," hoping that these will achieve understanding. Unfortunately, simple truths are likely to be half-truths.

In the striving for simplicity, ideas become abstract, all but meaningless in operational terms, and with little specific relationship to the actual experience of the people toward whom they are directed. Much of what passes for economic education deals with "individual rights," "property rights," "democracy," "freedom of opportunity." These ideas are among the most complex in our society; yet they are presented as "simple, self-evident truths." Moreover, there is a danger in discussions of *political* rights in an *economic* context, unless adequate steps are taken to make those rights fully valid and applicable in that context.

The second shortcoming, the penchant for using the techniques of salesmanship, comes naturally, perhaps, to businessmen who have worked out successful methods for selling merchandise. A common complaint of speakers at business meetings is that businessmen have done a far better job of selling their products than they have of selling themselves and their system, and the conclusion is usually drawn that the methods developed in the one field should be applied more vigorously and consistently in the other.

This line of thinking pushes the process of oversimplification still further, for sales promotional techniques can deal with only the simplest ideas and with only one idea at a time. The advertising profession long ago learned the limitations imposed by space and the attention span of the reader. But how successful can a two-page ad in a national magazine be in selling "free enterprise"? Or, for that matter, how effective can a course in "economic understanding" be which employs the techniques found useful in energizing a group of salesmen or dealers?

The selling approach is likely to create doubt and suspicion among those key outside publics about whose attitudes business is especially sensitive: writers, teachers, college professors, ministers, and other so-called "opinion formers." Such people are accustomed to dealing with ideas. They know that ideas have shadings and ramifications, that they are subject to qualification; they are alienated when these are ignored.

The methods of salesmanship are ill-designed to strengthen public acceptance and understanding of the business system. Generally speaking they can only seek to indoctrinate, not educate—and they do not even indoctrinate well. In any competitive struggle, it is necessary to appeal to the proper symbols. This is true for both products and allegiances. But the symbol systems are different for the two orders of "goods," a distinction often ignored by those seeking to sell free enterprise.

IV

Despite the difficulties of concept and execution which businessmen have experienced in their efforts to promote broader understanding of business, the need for such understanding remains. Because we live in a democracy, the integrity of the business system depends, in the final analysis, on its acceptance and support by all important groups within American society. Businessmen, after all, are a political minority. There are far more workers than there are employers, and there are millions of other citizens outside the business system proper who are also members of the electorate. In any test of political power at the polling place, businessmen, if they have only themselves to depend upon, will inevitably be the losers.

Generally speaking, the public has a much better understanding of other major social institutions than it has of business. There is a fairly good understanding of government, and of education, and of the church—at least in terms of essential functions and central characteristics. There is no comparable understanding of business.

The workings of the modern business system are not as easily grasped as in earlier days. No longer are there a few readily identified business establishments with sharply defined functions. No longer are there merely one or two or three steps between production and consumption. Division of labor has proceeded so far, and so many specialized activities have been developed, that today the workings of the system as a whole are difficult to visualize.

The diverse parts of the system, moreover, are intimately related. The functioning of any part is materially conditioned by the functioning of many other parts. Developments in one segment can have unpredictable repercussions throughout the system. Actions which may seem eminently desirable in their own right may have consequences that are far from salutary. Policies with painful immediate results may in the long run be beneficial to all concerned. If ours were a totalitarian society, action could be taken and policies pursued with much less concern as to whether or not they were generally understood. In a democracy, lack of public knowledge of economic processes can be a major hazard, not only for the business system but for society.

Under these circumstances, it is not only shortsighted but dangerous to promote biased, oversimplified, distorted versions of the workings of the business system. Much of what has been done thus far is of little value; some of it has been harmful. Much more searching and objective thought needs to be given the problem. For that matter, more effort needs to be made to define the problem.

Granted that there is need for broader public understanding

of economic affairs, how can it be achieved? How can we develop concepts which will reflect and explain the realities of modern economic life? How can these concepts, which are far from "simple and self-evident," be presented in a manner that will gain both understanding and affirmation? What groups need to be reached, and how? And how can all this be integrated into a broader appreciation of the democratic values that are implicit in the basic institutions of our society?

V

More is involved than public understanding of the economic system; confidence in business management itself is also necessary, and one does not inevitably follow from the other.

The successful operation of the American business system requires that broad powers be vested in the businessman. He must have freedom to act according to his best judgment, because anything that too narrowly restricts that freedom introduces elements of rigidity which may interfere with proper functioning. He must be able to make a sufficient rate of profit to maintain the strength of his enterprise, and he must have wide discretion in the way he uses those profits. He must have considerable freedom in the manner he organizes his undertaking and utilizes his work force, and he must have latitude in making judgments about people which may materially affect their livelihoods and futures. He must be free to deal with those he chooses and to make decisions which may have serious consequences for them. He must be free to make mistakes as well as to succeed, with possible results in either case extending far beyond himself or his immediate enterprise.

It is asking a great deal of any society to permit this degree of power and independent discretion to any group, for there is always the danger that it will be used capriciously or against the public interest. Such power will be tolerated only so long as society in general has confidence that it is not being used for narrowly selfish purposes. Anything which undermines that confidence is likely to lead to the imposition of controls which may lead eventually to serious impairment of the system. Such controls need not necessarily be governmental. Some of the most serious restrictions on the freedom of business judgment have come in recent years from organized labor.

A climate of public opinion favorable to the operation of the business system depends primarily, not on education as such, but on the integrity of management. People must be assured, not by words but by deeds, that the system is serving the needs of society at large. Business must be administered as a public trust, and people's experience with business must give them grounds for believing that this is an operative fact, not a pious platitude.

The key here is *experience*. How do people actually experience the business system? What is the nature of their contacts with it? In what ways and to what degrees does the system measure up to their expectations? There is always an important place for interpreting, for explaining, for broadening public understanding of business problems and objectives. But the actual experience of people with business is far more important than what anyone says about it.

This applies not only to efforts on the part of business leaders to create a favorable climate of opinion; it applies equally to efforts on the part of those antagonistic to business to destroy confidence in the business system. So long as business continues to do a good job, so long as it continues to meet the expectations and serve the needs of the American people, we need have little concern for the fulminations of anti-business elements. The danger lies not in the detractors of business but in the possibility that businessmen, through their shortcomings, will give these detractors concrete materials on which to build their case. If we keep our house in order, nothing the dissident elements say or do will be of much moment; if we do not, nothing *we* say or do will be of much avail.

The American way of life does not need to be *sold* so much as it needs to be *lived*. And among those who must do the "living" are businessmen themselves. It is not enough for business to perform its economic functions well, although this is of great importance. Business must also conform with and aid in strengthening the basic values of American society, which are strongly democratic. This requires that businessmen have a clear conception of their role in American society, that they operate their businesses on democratic principles, and that they assume their share of the broader responsibilities of citizenship in a free society. In a real sense, the basic problem is the attitudes and understanding of the businessmen themselves; public attitudes are secondary and largely derivative.

Chapter TWO

Basic Misconceptions

If the root problem of public confidence in business is the attitudes and understanding of businessmen themselves, it is important to examine some of their common assumptions as to the role of business. Such an examination reveals two basic misconceptions. The first of these is the justification of the business system largely in terms of its demonstrated ability to produce vast quantities of goods and services at prices great numbers of people can afford to pay; the second is the idea that business in the pursuit of its own self-interest automatically promotes the good of all, with the corollary proposition that anything which interferes seriously with the pursuit of business self-interest is contrary to the interests of society and somehow un-American.

I

Business has sought traditionally to justify itself by its contribution to a constantly improving standard of living for all groups in our society. America's thinking, its traditions—its entire history—have been geared to such improvement.

Yet, if management's only or chief justification for the continued exercise of power were the material well-being that the business system provides, it would not keep that power for long because there simply are not sufficient resources to meet the demands made upon it.

It has been characteristic of American life from the beginning that people have high expectations of it. Those who settled this country, first as colonists and later as immigrants, left the lands of their birth for our shores because they had hopes and aspirations which they thought could be realized here as nowhere else on earth. As a result, the American people probably have made stronger and more insistent demands for the good things of life, spiritual as well as material, than any other people in history. They have been willing to work for these things, because that too is an integral part of the American tradition. But they have also been impatient with people or institutions that seemed to frustrate their efforts or deny the validity of their aspirations.

The record of business on the score of material goods is impressive. It has created a standard of living not even remotely approached anywhere else on earth. That standard of living, moreover, is broadly shared; extremes of wealth and poverty that prevail elsewhere do not exist here. Differences in the comforts and amenities enjoyed by different economic groups are sufficient to provide incentives for ambition and effort but not so great as to divide our society into irreconcilably warring classes. On Sunday morning it is hard to tell the millionaire from the day laborer, and the sons of the two men may be roommates in college. This wide sharing of the fruits of our economic system is one of the major elements of its strength.

But public confidence depends on more than the maintenance of material prosperity. Unless this were the case, the business system as we know it could hardly have survived the

Great Depression and would be in jeopardy at every reverse in the economic trend. Economic growth is not constant, and never can be constant in a free society; a condition of free economic processes is periodic readjustment to restore necessary balance and to set the stage for further growth. The fact that the business system has thus far survived such readjustments—including more than one major dislocation of the economy—is a clear demonstration that survival involves more than economic factors per se.

The effort to justify the business system in terms of its material achievements suffers from a fatal weakness. Economic values are always relative—and subjective. If our measure of progress is improvement in the standard of living, we are using a rubber yardstick. In terms of the standards prevailing at any one time there will always be an "ill-housed, ill-clothed, ill-fed one third." The reliefer today lives better in material terms than the medieval king. But the reliefer compares his lot, not with standards that prevailed in another country or another generation but with the standards current in his own society.

That society will always be stratified because some degree of stratification is a necessary consequence of division of labor. Under Soviet communism, with all of its claims for a classless society, life is even more stratified than under American capitalism. In any such society, standards adopted by the higher strata come to be considered the norm. Anything falling markedly short of that norm is considered inadequate, substandard, impoverished. Thus no matter how much we may improve "objective" conditions, this improvement in itself can never alter the "subjective reality."

Consider, for example, the constant drive of unions for "more." Anyone who has followed the course of organized labor during the past twenty years must be impressed with its apparently insatiable drive for higher wages and improved benefits. No matter how great the concessions made one year, the demand for further concessions the next year is equally importunate; any given level of achievement is merely a platform, a starting point, for further demands.

Consider, too, the relativity of so-called "adequate" standards of living. What is considered a "minimum standard of health and decency" (to use the phraseology commonly found in state minimum wage laws) is likely to be based largely on current middle-class standards. For this reason, estimates of minimum living-standard requirements at any given time are almost always unrealistic in terms of the current distribution of worker incomes. In 1901 more than 40 per cent of worker families had incomes of less than $600 a year, the figure set as the minimum standard at that time. In 1909 about the same proportion of families earned less than the $850 then considered the minimum. In 1918 about 30 per cent had incomes less than the $1300 estimated as the cost of the minimum budget prepared by the Bureau of Labor Statistics. In 1935 some 60 per cent of non-relief workers earned less than the $1261 maintenance budget prepared by the Works Progress Administration. Even in prosperous 1948 between 30 and 40 per cent of worker families did not have sufficient income to provide the scale of living specified by the Bureau of Labor Statistics' City Workers' Family Budget.[1]

The persistence with which over a period of fifty years, even in relatively good times, between 30 and 40 per cent of workers' families lag behind successive reformulations of minimum budgets suggests the permanence of an "underprivileged third" of our population. But the point is that the standard of judging is constantly changing. Types of food, shelter, and clothing considered luxuries in one decade be-

[1] Dorothy S. Brady, "Scales of Living and Wage Earners' Budgets," *The Annals of the American Academy of Political and Economic Science,* March 1951, vol. 274.

come necessities a decade or so later; their lack becomes a matter of deprivation and in a social sense defines impoverishment.

Material progress alone is thus neither an adequate justification of the business system nor a sufficient guarantee of its public acceptance. This is not to imply that increasing the supply and quality of goods is unimportant. The effort to do so is properly a part of the businessman's concern, and the better and more widely distributed goods he makes possible are tangible evidence that the business system in fact tends to operate in the general interest.

Just as good rates of pay, and reasonable prospects for future increases, are among the necessary conditions for satisfactory employee relations, so are good and continuously improving products and services among the necessary conditions for stable relations between business and society. But neither pay nor material prosperity, however high they may be, can in themselves assure the climate of employee or public opinion in which management and the business system can perform most effectively.

II

A more subtle and complex misconception involves the idea of self-interest in business affairs. In actual practice, business has shown a broad measure of public responsibility and concern for human welfare. Business practice in this respect, however, is considerably better than business theory, at least as that theory is generally expressed.

According to classical economic doctrine, business is assumed to be conducted primarily for pecuniary gain. Modern theory has somewhat softened the bleak picture of "economic man," but the basic image remains relatively unchanged. The businessman himself generally explains his actions in terms of self-interest. This does not mean that he systematically ignores all interests other than his own. Especially with the rise of professional management and the emergence of the large, publicly owned corporation as the dominant form of economic activity, increased attention is being given to the impact of business decisions on the well-being of society. There is, moreover, a conscious effort to relate the needs of business to the needs of the community. Nevertheless, most businessmen are likely to insist that the primary purpose of business is to serve the self-interest of its owners and managers.

In classical doctrine as well as business ideology, the pursuit of self-interest is expected to redound to public good. In Adam Smith's formulation:

Every individual is continually exerting himself to find out the most advantageous employment for whatever capital he can command. . . . But this study of his own advantage naturally, or rather necessarily leads him to prefer that employment which is most advantageous to society . . . he is in this . . . led by an invisible hand to promote an end which was no part of his intention.

This theory is beautiful in its simplicity and ranks in the field of economic thought with Darwin's concept of the struggle for survival in the field of biology. Although considerably elaborated and qualified in its modern forms, it remains the basic rationale of the business system. Most emphatically, the theory does not subordinate public to private interests; essentially, it argues for their underlying harmony. But it is not only an oversimplification of the facts of modern economic life, it suffers from a moral weakness as well: it relieves the businessman from concern for the consequences of his actions on the assumption that "economic laws" will automatically transmute his self-seeking into public benefit.

Because of the influence of laissez-faire economics, the businessman has been encouraged to take a narrow and ex-

clusive view of his role in society. Nor does he seek to hide
or disguise his emphasis on self-interest as the central driving
force of the business system; on the contrary, he continually
calls attention to it. He may soften its harshness by emphasiz-
ing the idea of service, but he goes on to rationalize service
as itself a form of self-interest—as in the slogan, "He profits
most who serves best." And if he talks of *enlightened* self-
interest, he usually implies that he considers it superior to
narrow self-interest mainly because the broader sharing of
benefits helps make success more certain. Being enlightened
is simply being smart.

III

Self-interest, whether narrow or enlightened, is an unstable
basis on which to erect a system of economic institutions.
Institutions must be in harmony with what those who live
under them consider to be morally right, and there are
deeply ingrained elements in Western tradition (as well as
in the traditions of most civilizations) which hold selfishness
to be one of the cardinal sins.

In terms of Christian ethics, the effort to explain and
justify the workings of the business system on the basis of
self-interest is to glorify greed as obedience to higher social
law. Enlightened self-interest is subject to the same moral
strictures as narrow self-interest. There is always the critical
question of *intent,* because intelligent self-interest is still
selfishness; morally, it is on a footing with stupid self-interest.
Because of the insistence on a self-interest rationale, the
business system is placed, by its own defenders and apologists,
in moral conflict with the ethical foundations of its own
society.

Businessmen are among the few leadership groups in
history whose ethic has been frankly egoistic. The landed

gentry of England, the feudal nobility of France, and other ruling castes in ancient and modern times at least protested that their policies were in the interest of the general welfare, however much they may actually have been pursuing simple self-interest. Even the Communist party goes to great lengths to explain its policies in terms of their ultimate benefit to mankind.

The avowal of self-interest by the businessman has undeniable virtues. A certain amount of diffidence as to the magnanimity of one's motives is a good thing. Great and terrible have been the crimes committed against humanity in the name of humanity. The business ethic is not likely to lead to the kind of excesses into which people infected with a zeal for the good of mankind are often tempted.

Nevertheless, the straightforward avowal of self-interest has serious consequences, for it renders the businessman and the business system forever suspect. For one thing, it places a moral stigma on an essential business function: the making of profit. "Production for use, not for profit" is a recurrently popular slogan, especially in times of economic distress. The teacher, the minister—even the lawyer and doctor—are likely to view profit-making institutions with a degree of suspicion and to take pride that they are working for higher, more noble purposes. Nonprofit corporations are considered somehow superior to their commercial counterparts. Corporate profits are a favorite object of attack, especially by organized labor. Demands for higher wage rates are frequently justified by the claim that profits are too high and that owners and managers are growing rich at the expense of workers and the public. Periods of rising prices are always accompanied by charges of profiteering, an epithet which has acquired a host of unsavory meanings. The taxing of corporate profits is safe and often popular politics, and during periods of national emergency the taxation of "excess profits" comes near to being a

political necessity. Despite his awareness that profits are the
necessary basis for risk and expansion, the businessman himself is often defensive on the subject.

An American business leader recently lamented "the old
type-casting of the businessman as materialistic, selfish, and
insatiable in his pursuit of money." But if the public has an
image of businessmen as "narrowly and rapaciously selfish,
with no responsibility except to themselves and their owners,"
the businessman himself has largely created this caricature
by his own definition of his motives.

Apprehension over the businessman's self-avowed motives
is partly responsible for recurrent demands for more rigid
supervision and control of business by government. Americans are more concerned with the misuse of power than they
are with the possession of power. Given the businessman's
own emphasis on the central position of self-interest, people
inevitably look to government, in which they feel they have
a voice and which in theory is concerned for the good of all,
to make sure that business lives up to proper standards. Apprehension over business motives also underlies demands for
centralized planning and direction, especially in times of
crisis, despite the crippling and impoverishing effects which
may well ensue.

In fact, demands for more rigid government controls, public ownership, and the like are best understood in symbolic
rather than economic terms. Such demands usually have
little to do with technical needs, and may seriously complicate
administrative processes; rather, they grow out of a pervad-
ing sense of unease that affairs of vital public concern may
be conducted without due regard to the public welfare.

Economic stability often requires strong fiscal and administrative measures by government, which may be difficult or impossible to apply unless their painful consequences
can be accepted as necessary for the *general* good and not

merely for the good of "bankers," "Wall Street," and "big business." Likewise, the necessary adjustments which business enterprises must make from time to time (layoffs during periods of recession, displacement of workers by new machinery, insistence on discipline and productivity at the work place) must be accepted as part of the system and ultimately for the general good. The self-interest theory hampers such acceptance.

The dangers to business from such public suspicion are illustrated by the experience of certain Latin American countries where inflation has run wild, in large part because of unsound "welfare" programs and severe restrictions on business enterprise. In Europe the widespread appeal of socialism reflects an insistent demand that the vital processes of society be in the hands or under the control of government. In countries under Communist domination, the rise of communism, the seizure of power by a militant minority, and the subsequent abolition of private business enterprise were facilitated by the broad gulf which had grown up between business and the public.

The attractiveness of communism on ethical grounds for certain persons of high moral aspirations reflects their reaction against a business system which makes self-interest paramount. The strength of the appeal of both socialism and communism is indicated by the amount of socialist unworkability and the amount of Communist terror and violation of human rights their supporters are willing to tolerate for the sake of systems which at least give lip service to concern for mankind.

Communists and socialists play up the symbols of human welfare but neglect, and often violate, the reality. The American business system emphasizes the symbols of self-interest, but actually operates with substantial concern for human values. But such is the power of symbols in human affairs that people and systems are often taken at the face value they place on themselves. In this respect, socialism and communism are grossly oversold and the American business system grossly undersold—in each case by its own supporters.

The attractiveness of Soviet appeals for underdeveloped countries is enhanced by the distrust of those countries for private business institutions, largely as a result of their suspicion of the business ethic. Ideologically speaking, the free world is at a competitive disadvantage in the "struggle for men's minds." Despite Russia's record of unfulfilled promises and her attempts to use economic aid for purposes of subversion, the ethical appeal of Marxism is strong. Experience suggests that people are more likely to put up with privation imposed in the name of public good than with plenty generated as a by-product of self-interest.

In the field of foreign aid, our professions of self-interest have caricatured our noblest sentiments as self-seeking, and our most imaginative undertakings as the manipulation of less fortunate peoples for our own purposes. As a nation we are willing to make great sacrifices. But we cannot explain our willingness even to ourselves because of our commitment to self-interest—for how can self-interest be equated with, say, the willingness to give up life itself for a cause? And if we cannot fully understand our own motives, what about the beneficiaries of the sacrifice—say, the Europeans or the Asiatics for whom so many American lives have been paid forfeit in war?

But we need not go so far afield to find examples. Organized labor is one of the strongest groups in our society; yet despite its great power, it has been subjected to few controls. This is largely attributable to the fact that labor bases its case primarily on concern for the welfare of the working population. Unions are able to take with impunity many kinds of action, including economic coercion, which would be roundly condemned if taken by business. They escape effective criticism, however, because they are careful to define such action as incidental to the achievement of the union's expressed aim: the promotion of worker welfare.

Statements by labor leaders that "we're out for all we can get" are often applauded by important segments of the public—including those which tend to be critical of business. This attitude on the public's part reflects not only an acceptance of the claim that labor leaders are pursuing the interests of a sizable constituency but also a feeling that the businessman deserves whatever he gets, that since the businessman's own ethic is selfish anyone is welcome to anything he can get away with. And if self-interest is what makes the wheels go around, why should workers subordinate *their* self-interest to that of management?

IV

The concept of the role of self-interest in business processes needs to be reworked. As generally expressed it is neither an accurate description of the way things are nor a just appraisal of the motives behind most business decisions.

One of the earliest and most significant findings of human relations research was that workers are not motivated solely by economic considerations, that there are many so-called "nonlogical" factors (i.e., *noneconomically* logical factors) which condition their attitudes and behavior. It is curious that this insight has never been extended in any important way to business or management, that while it is now axiomatic that workers are complex and many-sided, management is still seen (and still thinks of itself) as the corporate embodiment of economic man. Yet managers, no less than workers, are members of groups that strongly influence their behavior, play roles that are socially defined, belong to a culture with a rich and elaborate system of values. Managers no more than workers are motivated solely by economic considerations. Managers in a word, are "human" too.

In business there has always been a system of *human* relations as well as a system of *economic* relations. To be sure, the two systems function in terms of two different and sometimes conflicting sets of values, with the result that there is often confusion as to the role the businessman is actually playing at any particular time. But just as with workers, owners and managers have never acted strictly in the terms ascribed to them by economic theory.

It is amusing to observe the extent to which the businessman will sometimes go in his efforts to explain in terms of self-interest an action which he wants to take for quite different reasons, some of which may be generous and unselfish. Because generosity and unselfishness are explicitly excluded from the frame of reference within which the businessman, *as a businessman,* is supposed to operate, he feels it necessary to explain himself in other terms. "Enlightened self-interest" is one such term. The frequency with which enlightened self-interest is appealed to reflects the difficulty of relating certain acts to self-interest at all.

Modern corporate philanthropy, for example, is typically explained as a means of promoting good will, although the real motivation may well be simply a sense of corporate responsibility. Employee benefit plans are usually justified on the basis of their presumed effect on productivity, although anyone experienced in personnel management can testify that genuine concern for employee welfare is often the compelling factor. Management has a legitimate interest in fostering good will and improving productivity; it also has a human interest in "doing what is right," although it is often reluctant to say so.

In any event, the justification of generous acts in terms of self-interest, whether "enlightened" or otherwise, helps soothe the businessman's conscience for acting contrary to his socially defined role—or, perhaps more accurately, helps reconcile the requirements of this role as a businessman and the requirements of his role as a citizen.

This circumlocution also helps make the action more palatable to those who benefit from it. Workers, for example, would be suspicious if a generous act were presented as anything other than self-interest. They, too, know the behavior appropriate to management's classic role and are likely to feel uncomfortable—and perhaps resentful—unless the act is defined in terms of that role. Their own classic role as workers, in turn, makes them dislike being indebted to management for favors. The situation reminds one of a father and son who go to great lengths of gruffness to hide their affection for each other and who would be fearfully embarrassed if that affection should ever inadvertently be expressed in words.

V

Although in actual practice the self-interest principle is muted, whether by "enlightenment," integration of roles, or otherwise, the fact that self-interest remains the generally recognized norm of business conduct has serious practical consequences.

It means that in critical situations businessmen are likely to be governed by this norm rather than by what may well be their real sentiments or by the norms of their nonbusiness roles. Who you think you are determines what you do in tight places. Under such circumstances, pressures both internal and external to conform with the expectations of business-role behavior are likely to be great, and the businessman may find himself doing things that in ordinary circumstances he would be reluctant to do.

Furthermore, in critical situations society is likely to take business at its word and turn for leadership to others, such as government or unions, whose norms of conduct at least *pro forma* include concern for the general welfare. This has happened before, as during the last Great Depression; it could happen again in future crises. What happens during crises, of course, is the critical test of leadership.

We are in need of norms which will take much more fully into account the real sentiments of American managers and businessmen, which are, like those of their countrymen, based on Judeo-Christian ethics. We need norms that recognize the multiple rather than unitary roles that businessmen play in actual life. We need to reinforce the businessman's ethical concerns, not neutralize them. We must make it appropriate for businessmen, even in the tightest situations, to act with all the complexity of their character in ways that may be tolerated normally but are now expected to fade before strictly economic considerations when the going gets rough.

We need a set of norms which will not serve as a cloak behind which selfishness can hide but will highlight deviations from the Judeo-Christian mode of conduct. For egoism in any guise is a form of idolatry, the worship of self. It will no doubt always be present, but it should not enjoy the immunity conferred by official sanction.

The harmony between individual and general interests is more profoundly true than classical theory imagined—but in reverse. It is not that individual selfishness makes for general good but that *unselfishness* makes for *personal* good. Classical theory is a travesty on Christ's teaching that he who would save his life must lose it.

Chapter THREE

Toward a Modern Theory of Enterprise

The picture of the business system usually presented to the
world is not only contrary to the realities of modern life but
leaves business, especially big business, open to attack on
its own premises. It fails to do justice to the facts and potentialities of the new and dynamic form of capitalism which
has evolved in America; and it fails to do justice to the real
sentiments and motivations of businessmen themselves.

We are badly in need of a theory, a rationale, which will
more adequately reflect and explain the modern system of
American capitalism and the place of the businessman in it.
We need a rationale that will be a guide and a norm for businessmen, that will effectively relate business to the rest of
society, and that will provide a solid foundation for public
confidence and trust.

Such a theory will recognize that business is a social organ
with functions far beyond the mere promotion of material
prosperity, and with motivations far broader than simple
self-interest. It will give consideration to the pervasive influence of religious forces in American life, the profound
consequences of the rise of the large, publicly owned corpo-

ration, and certain unique features of American historical development. It will, in other words, shake off outmoded economic doctrine and take a fresh look at the truth about today's business.

I

From its beginning, American society has been a religious and deeply moral society. In such a society people judge the actions and policies of business, government, organized labor, and all other institutions in moral terms: whether they are *right,* whether they are *fair,* whether they are *just.* Americans are highly critical of actions or policies that are based solely on rationality or practicality. And because American businessmen too are "American," they apply moral standards to their own conduct and respond sensitively to criticisms based on moral judgments. Businessmen themselves would be the first to agree that their most important problems are ethical rather than technical.

The ideas of fair play and self-restraint are essentially religious. They help keep dog-eat-dog practices in check and enable the business system to operate without strict governmental control; self-restraint rather than legal restraint is the rule. The typical emphasis on individual responsibility is another example of a basically religious idea which permeates American life, including business life.

Even from the earliest days the founders of American industrial enterprises were likely to be motivated not only by the prospects of material gain but also by a real desire to make goods and services more widely available to people in all walks of life. The idea of business as the source of material prosperity for everyone may have failed to take account of subjective realities, but it was not without idealism. The American concept of the mass market is not only an economic concept but an ethical concept as well; to miss its ethical content is to miss its real significance and the source of its real power.

American managers from the earliest days of the factory system have been concerned with the impact of that system on the society around them. They have been concerned with overcrowding in the larger cities and the growth of slums with all their attendant evils, with the assimilation of immigrants, with the problems of unemployment and insecurity. Businessmen have tried to deal with problems such as these not only as managers working within the structure of the enterprise but as citizens working within the broader structure of the community. The vast proliferation of voluntary welfare and civic agencies which is so striking a feature of American life is largely the creation of businessmen and their wives. Modern management is giving increasing recognition to its responsibilities to the community and the public, not merely as a means of promoting the good will of potential customers but from a sense of obligation for the welfare of others. Quite clearly, the motivations behind such actions have substantial ethical as well as economic content.

Many men of business hold sincere religious aspirations which they seek to realize in their business as well as their personal lives. The old dichotomy between private life and business life is disappearing. No longer can it be said, as once it was said, that a businessman in his private life might be a good husband and father, a conscientious citizen, and a devout churchman but so far as his business affairs were concerned the values of family life, of citizenship, and of religion applied only with significant reservations. These values find expression in business life—incompletely and unevenly, perhaps, but in appreciable degree.

It is not difficult to cite instances where ethical norms have been violated in business practice, or where they have been

observed more in the form than in the substance. But especially during the past quarter century business has come to
display a marked sense of public responsibility, a sense of
stewardship, which is in part a consequence of the development of professional management but more fundamentally a
reflection of a pervasive concern for ethical values.

We have here, however, a strange anomaly: while Judeo-
Christian ethics have deeply infused the institutions of our
society, including the institution of business, they have done
so in a secular rather than in a religious guise. We recognize
moral imperatives, but we are inclined to ascribe to them a
social origin and sanction rather than to recognize their religious roots. We bow to the demands of rightness, of fairness,
of justice; we affirm the dignity of man and the integrity of
the individual; we acknowledge the priority of human values.
But we conceive these things in social rather than in sacred
terms.

The ethic which guides our lives comes to us through a
secular filter. Herein is a source of danger. For while the
process lets through the form it screens out the essence.
While man's obligations to man come through with relative
clarity, man's obligations to God are obscured. Concern for
our fellow man comes to be seen as a matter of social convenience rather than as a consequence of brotherhood under
the fathership of God. We come to see unfairness and in-
justice as violative of social values rather than as trespasses
on divine commandments. We come to conceive of responsibility as sanctioned by the requirements of living together
rather than as accountability to our Heavenly Father.

This is not to deny the good which comes, in the business
world and elsewhere, from socially sanctioned behavior. But
if we look to and recognize only the social sanctions and
forget their divine origin, we cut ourselves off from our
spiritual wellsprings. Our codes of conduct become increas-

ingly arid because they have lost contact with that from which they derive their vitality and strength. To paraphrase Toynbee, efforts that are beneficent when exerted in the service of religion become demonic when dissociated from religion and an end in themselves.

We need to define, much more clearly and explicitly than we have yet defined it, the intimate relation between a man's religious faith and what he does in his business. We need to demonstrate that religion is just as relevant to the individual in his office as in his home or church. Especially do we need to establish explicitly understood Christian principles for the decision makers of business, the officers and executives entrusted with the conduct of business affairs. This is a task in which the theologian and the preacher must lead. They will find many helpers and followers in the world of business, devout men deeply troubled and seeking greater relevance between their work and their faith.

II

Any adequate theory of enterprise must also take into account the rise of the large, publicly owned corporation. Big business is not merely small business writ large; it is a new order of being and cannot be intelligently explained by concepts drawn from the experience of a small-enterprise economy. Two points in particular require attention: the drastic modification in the role of profits and the emergence of professional management.

The greater part of economic activity today is carried on by corporations rather than by a large number of individual entrepreneurs. Ours is a large-business economy, not only in terms of the share of the total economy accounted for by big business but in terms of the influence of big business in

all phases of economic life. The large enterprise is the proto-
type, the representative institution of the economy today.

One of the most significant consequences of this development is the separation of ownership from control in the affairs of enterprise. Owners—i.e., stockholders—generally are
too widely diffused to exercise control of the corporation.
Legally, of course, they have the final say, and management
is accountable *pro forma* to its stockholders for its stewardship. Actually, as anyone who has ever attended a stockholders' meeting can testify, their degree of control is tenuous.

In practice the typical stockholder of a major corporation
seldom behaves like an "owner." He is a necessary figure in
corporate life but not an active participant. He does not
have the sense of responsibility that is generally associated
with ownership, as in the case of a house or a farm or a small,
one-man business. His interest is chiefly an investment interest: he is concerned with the rate of dividend, the prospects
for capital appreciation, and the degree of speculative risk.
He has little "loyalty" for any particular corporation, and
readily shifts his investments from one to another as his own
judgment or his investment advisor's counsel may dictate.
The shareholder prospers largely by knowing when to buy
and sell, and is only indirectly concerned with profits as such.
He may be said to operate in terms of a profit motive, but the
profits are his, not the corporation's.

The managers of the corporation, on their part, cannot be
said to be actuated by a profit motive in the classical sense
because of their relatively small ownership. While they are
responsible for the profits of their corporation, these profits
accrue to the business and not to the managers except to the
extent of their typically minor ownership interests. The corporation is a legal entity without psychological motivations of
its own. It is the managers who have motives, but under

modern corporate organization these can be described as "profit motives" only by doing violence to the term itself.

This is not to suggest that managers are not interested in profits; quite the contrary. With the growth of professional management the top executive's status in the business world, the respect in which he is held by his fellow businessmen, depends in considerable part on the profitability of the enterprise under his management. As surgeons admire the skill of a fellow surgeon or lawyers the brilliance of a colleague's brief, so professionals in management esteem the acumen of their fellow professionals, usually as reflected in their financial statements.

One of the important functions of profits is to serve as a standard for evaluating the performance of managers. But within the structure of the enterprise itself, managers progress in terms of their ability to serve all the needs of the corporation as an on-going institution, not only the need for profits. And the manager's rewards are not limited to money. They are likely to take the form of improvements in position and status, as well as the satisfactions which come from a sense of achievement, power, and responsibility.

Furthermore, while advancement in the hierarchy carries with it improvement in the manager's income—with all that means in terms of economic security, creature comforts, and position in the community—wealth as such no longer enjoys the prestige or exerts the attraction it once did. The phenomenon of "conspicuous consumption" is much less apparent today than it was fifty or seventy-five years ago, when the businessman, generally lacking a place within a stable and established hierarchy that would help define his status, turned to flamboyant ways to demonstrate his achievement and establish his position. This kind of behavior is no longer necessary, and would be out of place among executives in most modern corporations. Now that the larger enterprise has become the dominant form of economic organization, position in the community is determined not so much by wealth as by position in the enterprise.

All this is far afield from the classical conception of the profit motive. The owner-manager of a small enterprise may function in terms of that conception, but it is neither an adequate nor an accurate description of the motivations of the professional managers of large, publicly owned corporations.

The first responsibility of the enterprise is for economic performance. This is its social function and its only social justification. Under modern conditions economic performance requires organization, and organization requires stability and continuity. Thus in a realistic sense the modern corporation is run not for its "owners" but for the enterprise itself.

This fact has profoundly altered the role of profit. Stability and continuity are much more important than making maximum profits on individual transactions. One of the worst sins a corporate management can commit is to make a high rate of profit at the cost of jeopardizing the company's long-range interests. Even at the expense of current profits, competent managements are expected to spend adequate sums on maintenance and replacement, on new and improved machinery, on research, and on many other activities designed to assure the organization's continued strength and vitality. By adding a time dimension, the rise of the modern corporation has created a new situation. The standard is no longer the maximizing of profits but the continuity of the enterprise.

The corporation must be run in such a way as to survive all vicissitudes: technological change, shifting markets, competition, vagaries in demand, inflation and depression, managerial error, legal complications, labor disputes, management succession. Emphasis must be placed on long-term planning of finance, productive facilities, organization, and marketing.

Buying and pricing policies must be devised in terms of the requirements of stability and continuity in buying and selling relationships. All of this may mean the maximizing of long-range rather than short-range profit, but this is not the essential point. What is essential is the corporation's need for survival, to which may be appended the role of profit in providing the means of survival.

In the modern corporation, profit is no longer a reward to one of the factors of production. Typically, only a portion of earnings is paid out to stockholders. The amount set aside for dividends is likely to be determined on the basis of "socially approved" rates of return—i.e., enough to maintain stockholder interest and preserve a ready market for the corporation's securities. A major portion of earnings is usually retained to aid in meeting the company's capital needs, among the most important of which are expansion, replacement, and improvement of productive facilities. Profits are thus a means of providing for the future—not merely the future of the corporation but of society. And because the needs of the future are great, profits must be correspondingly large if the corporation is to continue to perform its economic function effectively.

Unfortunately, this relationship between profits and survival is little understood. The social stake in profits is heavily obscured by the implicit equating of profit with self-interest. This confusion of the two concepts is not only inaccurate; it places the business system in a vulnerable moral position and seriously weakens the businessman's claims to leadership and the claims of the business system for social policies that will foster its efficient performance. A more realistic and more defensible doctrine of profits will have to be built around the survival needs of the enterprise as an instrumentality of social service.

III

The professional manager wields power and exercises authority within the enterprise by virtue not of ownership but of position. The circumstances of the large corporation necessarily emphasize the concepts of managerial trusteeship, service, and long-range planning and at the same time minimize personal acquisition and self-aggrandizement. Individual cleverness and ingenuity no longer win immediate cash rewards, as was often the case with owner-managers. The important considerations today are necessarily long-term, both for the corporation and the individual. This is a tendency, not an absolute condition. But even as a tendency it is a change of major significance.

Under a system of professional management people hold their positions and win advancement on a basis of merit and competence rather than through nepotism or ownership. This too is an important cultural change; for the fact—sometimes the accident—of kinship or ownership does not necessarily imply ability. The practices of the modern corporation are more likely than traditional arrangements to place high responsibility in the hands best qualified to exercise it.

An essential characteristic of any profession is recognition of responsibility beyond immediate personal interests. As management has grown more professional it too is growing increasingly aware of its responsibilities. Professional managers are coming to recognize that business can no longer pursue its economic interests regardless of social consequences. The big company in particular has developed into a quasi-public institution and as such has social and economic responsibilities beyond those of small companies. More and more the managers of big business are becoming aware that the welfare of their companies and of the business system itself are indissolubly bound up with that of the American economy and society. When such men express the faith that in the long run the good of society and the good of business go hand in hand, there may sometimes be a certain confusion as to which comes first; but of the strength and reality of the identification there can be no doubt.

Unless the policies of business—especially big business—benefit society they will not in the long run benefit business, no matter how attractive they may be in the short run. Socially irresponsible action is also economically irresponsible action—and vice versa. In either case irresponsible action not only does not pay but may have disastrous consequences for society *and* the company. Acting responsibly is not merely "doing the right thing" but doing what the needs and interests of the business *as a social institution* demand.

This is a far cry from classical theory which looked to the interplay of a multitude of individual self-interests to achieve a balance that would both protect and serve the public interest. A modern theory of enterprise must recognize the manner in which the internal dynamics of the corporation itself work toward such a balance. More important, it must emphasize the professional obligation of managers to protect and serve the public interest, not as a fortuitous by-product but as an integral part of their managerial function.

IV

Another major factor which must be considered in formulating a rationale of modern enterprise is the influence of certain unique features of American historical experience. The large-scale corporation is not peculiar to America, nor is America alone in its concern for religious and ethical values; these are factors which helped shape economic arrangements abroad as well as here. But American business has developed within an historical environment that has differed in important respects from that of other countries, and some of the distinguishing characteristics of American business life can be understood only by reference to these differences.

One such factor of great significance has been our broad domestic market. The American factory system grew up within an economy in which workers, consumers, and the public were all the same people. The genius of Henry Ford lay not only in his concept of mass production. Perhaps his most lasting contribution was his recognition of the fact that the best way to expand the markets for mass production was to improve the capacity of workers to consume. This was a natural conclusion to be drawn from the conditions of the American economy; it was a conclusion which could not be reached nearly so readily in economies built largely on industries serving export markets.

A further distinctive feature has been our strong emphasis on the virtues of competition. The Sherman Anti-Trust Act of 1890 and the Clayton and Federal Trade Commission acts of 1914 have been decisive factors in the flexibility, the dynamism, and the potentiality for growth which are characteristic of business in America today. They have forced management to be constantly alert to serving the public interest, rather than merely protecting its own. Not less important, they have given the public grounds for confidence in the efficacy of self-regulating economic processes and have made unnecessary the extremes of government intervention and control which the absence of enforced competition has made inevitable elsewhere.

But the most significant of the historical influences which have helped shape American business have to do with labor. Concern for good employee relations is a distinguishing characteristic of American industry, and business leaders spend a great deal of time and money in the effort to promote good relations within the enterprise. There may be considerable disagreement as to the best way to go about improving relations, but there is no disagreement with the proposition that good relations between management and men are a positive good in themselves. This attitude is an outgrowth of certain peculiarities in the history and traditions of the country.

American business enterprise has been faced with a persistent shortage of labor. Whereas in other countries (for example, Great Britain a century and a half ago and India today) industrialization has generally arisen under conditions of large-scale labor surplus, American managers, with only occasional and temporary exceptions, have had to build and maintain their enterprises in the face of chronic labor scarcity. The ever-expanding frontier and the free availability of land slowed down the drift of workers from the farms to the cities. At the same time the expansion of the frontier increased the demand for the products of industry. The resulting shortage of labor was somewhat but by no means wholly relieved by immigration. In consequence the American industrialist from colonial times forward was constrained to give thought to the welfare of his workers to a degree that seldom occurred to his European contemporaries.

The special American penchant for mechanization reflects the need for conserving the available supply of labor. The special American genius for organization reflects the need for utilizing scarce skills in the most effective manner possible. Likewise, the special American concern for maintaining good relations with employees reflects the necessity for making employment as attractive as possible to people who are in a position to pick and choose among places of work. It makes a profound difference—psychological as well as technical—whether workers are easily come by or hard to find and keep. Scarcity always enhances value—and respect. And that which

is valued and respected is better cared for, particularly when
lack of care may lead to loss. Scarcity has conditioned the
minds of workers as well as managers. Just as American
workers have grown to expect and demand good wages, they
have grown to expect and demand good treatment. This, too,
has strongly conditioned the thinking of realistic managers.

Another and more subtle factor that has helped sharpen
the interest of American managers in the quality of their employee relations is their rather ambivalent attitude toward
their own authoritarian role in the hierarchy of industrial
organization. The lack of a high degree of social stratification in this country, the relative ease with which people have
been able to move from one social class to another, and above
all the strong egalitarian elements in American culture have
tended to deprive members of the managerial group of a full
sense of assurance in the rightness of their authority. Where
lines between social classes are more definitely drawn, authority tends to be exercised as a matter of unquestioned right, and
to be so accepted by the workers themselves. Americans, on
the contrary, are troubled by vague feelings of unease when
placed in positions where they must behave in ways of superiority toward other Americans who by all standards of the
American tradition are their equals and whose position of
inferiority in the business enterprise in no way detracts from
their essential equality as citizens and men.

This unease helps explain the peculiar sensitivity of the
American employer to what his employees think of him—as
expressed, for example, in his widespread use of such devices
as "morale surveys" and employee opinion polls. But while
this sensitivity and the use of such devices may be a source
of wonder or amusement to foreign observers, they reflect an
important characteristic of American industrial life: the conflict between a deep-seated egalitarianism and the functional

necessity for a certain degree of authoritarianism in relationships within the industrial organization.

These feelings of unease are likely to be particularly strong when "good native Americans" find themselves in positions of authority over other "good native Americans." The same compunctions are often strikingly absent, by contrast, when the "good native Americans" are in positions of authority over less favored groups, such as Negroes or recent immigrants. In such relationships, the American manager is more likely to think and act in ways similar to his counterparts in other societies that take for granted the prerogatives of members of "superior" classes to command their "inferiors." Superordination in such cases is not merely functional; it implies and assumes that the superiors are also *better men*.

This tendency to differentiate in attitudes toward subordinates according to their social and ethnic characteristics goes far toward explaining some of the seeming contradictions in the history of American industrial relations. For despite the concern for employee good will postulated above as a distinguishing feature of American management, this country has been torn by some of the bloodiest and most intractable labor strife of any modern nation. Much of this strife has arisen, however, in industries which have employed large numbers of immigrant laborers: steel, mining, and automobiles, for example. Here, stresses and strains of emerging large-scale enterprise and conflicts of economic interest were further and often intolerably aggravated by the conflict of cultures, the lack of adequate means of communication, and a widespread feeling on the part of owners and managers that their laborers were "naturally" inferior.

It is significant that many of the early concepts of management-labor relations first developed in the large-scale enterprises which employed large numbers of immigrant workers. This is especially clear in the work of Frederick W. Taylor.

But management was not the only party affected; among the immigrants themselves, attitudes of distrust and patterns of conflict and antagonism that they brought from abroad were perpetuated and persist in some degree to this day. The children of the immigrant workers, and *their* children, often grew up in families and neighborhoods where the unfairness and harshness of bosses was taken for granted and a basic conflict between the interests of management and the interests of labor was conceived as a natural law.

The tide of European immigration thus left a permanent imprint on industrial relations in America, not only through its influence on management thinking but more importantly through the manner in which resulting management practices conditioned the attitudes and outlook of what came to be a substantial segment of the working class, the immigrants and their descendants.

By now the wheel of history has turned another full cycle, and the sons and grandsons and great-grandsons of the once "inferior breeds" are fully as "good" and "native" and "American" as those of the men for whom their forebears worked. And their bosses are beset by the traditional feelings of diffidence. It is not without significance that the modern "science of human relations," which has won such wide attention in management circles, first emerged in the mid-thirties—about the time the last wave of immigration began to be fully digested.

Neither is it without significance that at this same time the labor movement in this country entered into the period of phenomenal growth which has made it so powerful a factor in modern industrial life. For by then the labor force was composed of people who had acquired the elements of American culture, who demanded to be treated as self-respecting, upstanding American citizens, and who sometimes found their deepest sentiments violated by management attitudes and practices which were a carry-over from an earlier period. And so they revolted and sought to create through the device of unions the means for enforcing the respect and consideration which they had grown up to expect as their due.

This is not the place to examine the extent to which the union movement may have substituted one form of arbitrary authority for another. Suffice it for our purposes to note that this "revolt of labor" was deeply shocking to management. Among other things, it hastened the change in management's attitudes which was already under way but had not moved fast enough to keep pace with the "Americanization" of the labor force.

But the external pressures of the union movement, the exigencies of a scarce supply of labor, and a peculiar sensitivity to worker attitudes growing out of the egalitarian American tradition do not entirely explain the special concern for good employee relations which is characteristic of American management. To these must be added management's own search for a better way of life for itself and its employees.

American history from its earliest beginnings has been instinct with the search for better ways of life; not merely better ways of earning a livelihood but better ways of *living*. One means by which that characteristic expresses itself is the value placed by management on being "a good employer." The public evaluation of an enterprise is often based largely on its reputation in this respect. Businessmen take pride in having their firms known as "good places to work," not only by workers but by the general public and their fellow businessmen; in formulating their business policies, they are likely to take this factor very much into account. This is not a new development but a feature of our entire industrial history.

This historical theme has been expressed in a variety of ways: in utopian ventures a century and more ago to "uplift" the economic and intellectual status of workers; in the development of the now outmoded concept of "welfare capitalism"; in the introduction of a wide variety of employee benefit plans—group insurance and hospitalization, profit sharing, paid vacations and holidays, retirement allowances, paid sick leave, regularized employment, and a host of other measures designed to provide greater present and future security for workers and their families. Measures such as these were not the inventions of the unions; they were originally developed and installed by managements, usually at their own initiative and of their own free will, in an effort to assist in meeting the needs of workers in modern industrial society. The unions have taken these plans over as their own and considerably extended their application, but in doing so they have merely followed a pattern already well established by progressive, forward-looking managements.

Critics of management have always viewed management-sponsored programs such as these with skepticism, not so much in terms of the scales of benefits provided—although these have not gone without challenge—as in terms of the motivations behind them. The union's interest in employee benefit plans is looked upon as straightforward and understandable; but why should management be concerned? The very fact that it is concerned is looked upon as prima facie evidence that management has something more in mind than merely the welfare of its employees. Here again, management's own professed logic of self-interest casts a pall of doubt over what might well be neither more nor less than genuine concern for the people associated with management in a common enterprise.

The special concern of American businessmen and managers for good employee relations may be accounted for in a variety of ways. But it owes its unique character to the egalitarian American tradition, and the simple desire of those in strategic positions within the business system to create an industrial way of life that comports with their sense of the fitness of things.

Part **TWO**

The Political Economy of Industrial Organization

Chapter FOUR

Freedom Within *Enterprise*

If we accept the premise that the attitudes of people toward business are largely a product of their experience with business, employee relations assume a vital significance. The most intimate experience most people have with the business system comes through being employees. The quality of their relations with management and with each other, the extent to which their work is satisfying and rewarding, will in large measure determine not only their attitude toward their immediate employer but their attitude toward the business system as a whole.

But the problem is broader. How business is run has an enormous influence on how society operates. Business is more than an economic system: it is a political economy, a government of men brought together for economic purposes. Business and government are closely similar in their most essential aspects: both are organizations of human beings and both depend, in the long run, on the creative intelligence and effort and on the voluntary support and acceptance of the people who comprise them. Economic organization is simply one type of political organization; it is not a different order of being but a subclass of a general order. When business ignores this truth it endangers not only its own well-being but the well-being of society.

From our beginnings as a nation the people of this country have been concerned with the problems of human freedom. In the simple, agrarian society of an earlier day, these problems were largely external to the business enterprise. The great issues were largely Constitutional and legal: freedom of religion and the press, equal protection of the laws, freedom of contract, universal suffrage. When the individual or the family was the productive unit—whether on the farm or in the handicraft shop—laws were a reasonably sufficient guarantee of personal freedom. But as economic relations and economic organization have grown more complex, laws alone are no longer enough. Many legal and Constitutional issues are still not fully resolved, but now in addition to these there are other problems which must be worked out within the enterprise itself if our continuing concern for human freedom is to be served. Freedom is no longer merely a matter of governmental policy; it is now a matter of business policy as well.

Today most people work for a living as members of organizations. Their personal experience as employees profoundly affects their outlook on the world around them and on life in general. The extent to which employees in industry have an opportunity to develop and use their potentials as individuals and as members of cooperating groups largely determines the caliber of the persons comprising the society. We cannot have a democratic society if so large a section as that represented by industry is run in an authoritarian manner. Business, in the way it is run, can support and strengthen democracy or seriously undermine it.

Furthermore, as the following chapters seek to demonstrate, methods of organization and administration based on concepts of personal liberty are the most efficient for the business enterprise itself. This is not a case of conflict between the interests of business and the interests of society. It is not even a matter of enlightened self-interest, but an example of real correspondence of interests. Management's ability to apply the principles of liberty in the conduct of its affairs greatly enhances the effectiveness of its leadership both inside and outside the organization, and is the real test of its fitness to survive and prosper in a democracy.

One of the most remarkable facts of world history has been the achievements of democratic capitalism during the past one hundred and fifty years, particularly in America. The basis of these achievements has been largely the release of creative, productive energies made possible by free political and economic institutions. These facts are widely recognized. Yet one of the ironies of modern times is the failure to see the full implications of the free enterprise system for the internal conduct of business affairs. Business eagerly defends the free economic process against the stifling effect of too much government control, but often fails to see that the essential principles advocated for government apply equally to the organization and administration of business, and that the violation of these principles produces within business itself the same stifling results, the same frustration of spontaneous productive energy, that their violation in the larger field of government policy produces within the general economic system.

Perhaps the greatest challenge of modern times is for creative business leadership which can develop within industry itself the methods of democratic organization and control which have been worked out for the political state. Obviously, this is no easy task. Political institutions cannot be taken over intact by business. Business cannot be run by the ballot box or by a Congress. We must develop other inventions, adapted to the special circumstances of business, which will give to employees at all levels of our economic organization a greater sense of personal participation, a greater sense of belonging, a greater sense of dignity and recognition for their worth as individuals and as respected members of the industrial community.

II

Businessmen are inclined to assume that the form of business organization is dictated by the needs of the job. While this is part of the truth, it is seldom the whole truth. How a business is organized is an expression, however unconscious, of the management's attitude toward the people under it. Like a political democracy, an organization democracy reflects the conviction that people are capable of initiative and responsibility, of intelligent judgment and the ability to adapt to changing situations. Conversely, an authoritarian organization reflects an assumption of management that its subordinates are incapable of acting wisely without rigid supervision from above.

In this connection there is a significant affinity between the welfare state, managerial paternalism, and certain elements of trade unionism. Each is authoritarian. In each case, external authority seeks to determine what people need and what they should want—and this applies to certain managements, certain politicians, and certain unions. In all three cases, the basic attitude is one of contempt for people. People are not seen as creatures with their own rights, aspirations, and potentialities, but rather as hewers of wood or casters of ballots; objects to be enticed, cajoled, and if necessary coerced into serving the needs of authority.

Certain businesses today resemble the authoritarian state. All direction, all thinking, all authority tends to flow from the top down. While the top administrator may delegate certain parts of his responsibility to those at lower levels, he is merely authorizing them to implement and effectuate policies and directives he has set up. While the over-all directive may be broken down into a series of parts and parceled out to different people, and while these people may be expected to show initiative, drive, and judgment in executing their work, their activity is essentially carrying out orders.

To make such an organization work, management is forced to set up a rigorous system of controls to see that things get done and to insure that people do not make too many mistakes. A minimum of reliance is placed on the people in the organization, and the system depends primarily on the initiative and judgment of those at the top.

An inevitable corollary is the elaboration of staff organizations; for if the exercise of judgment and skill is largely reserved to top administrators, they must be assisted by specialists. The result is a further extension of controls through the staff departments, as well as a complication of the organization structure, thus leading to the necessity for more controls to hold the organization together and make it work. At the same time, because of the necessity for operating the controls and because people at each successive level must be supervised and directed in their work, the supervisory hierarchy becomes more and more extended.

What are some implications of this situation for the people in the organization? Staff specialists and higher levels of management, feeling that supervisors cannot be trusted to use good judgment at all times (and by "good judgment" they mean what they themselves would do under the circumstances), are impelled to establish precise rules to govern every contingency, or to appropriate broad areas of responsibility—all for the purpose of guarding against the possibility that supervisors or line executives may "make mistakes." Certainly, some broad framework of policy is necessary within which the supervisor should be required to work, but the danger lies in substituting elaborate bureaucratic controls for the good judgment which should arise from the supervisor's own intimate knowledge of immediate situations. Even more serious is the effect of such minute controls in undermining the initiative of supervisors, so that ultimately their judgment really cannot be trusted because they have never had a chance to use it.

What is the effect of this system on rank-and-file workers? There is considerable evidence on this score in the frequent complaints of management itself over the apathy of employees, their lack of initiative, their lack of interest in the affairs and problems of the enterprise, their antagonism to management. Rather than blame this state of affairs on agitators, or on faults in the educational system, or on errors in modern methods of raising children, certain managements need only look within their own organizations.

The attempt to use people as *means* rather than as *ends*—which is characteristic of the authoritarian organization—alienates employees from unity with management in the productive process. Their own labor becomes to them likewise a means: something alien to their real purposes and interests; something through which to procure the good things of life, rather than a good in itself; something to be given sparingly, as a cost.

A further and serious consequence of authoritarian administration is its tendency to inhibit the adaptiveness and problem-solving ability of the organization. Because judgment and initiative flow from the top down and because of elaborate systems of supervision and control, those at the lower levels gradually lose their ability to solve the problems which confront them and their capacity to adapt to new situations. The processes of adaptation and problem solving thus tend to move to higher levels in the organization. As problems become more complex—often because they have been incompletely solved —corrective action must be taken at higher and higher levels and eventually must be dealt with at the top of the management hierarchy. But this upward movement does not stop even at the top of the organization. It tends to move right out of the organization itself to the level of the trade association or its equivalent, and from there often keeps right on moving until it comes to rest in the government.

All of this has profound significance for democracy. When the methods of business organization increase the psychological dependency of its members—workers and executives alike—they hinder the processes of individual growth and development basic to democracy. Under these circumstances, significant numbers of workers (as well, be it noted, as executives) inevitably look about for someone to lean on, someone who can provide magical solutions to their problems, leaders who can point the way out—or, in more purely psychological terms, someone who can play the role of the good father and resolve the difficulty for his children. Since this is a role that management is poorly suited to play, employees turn to others—typically politicians and labor leaders. This kind of solution not only creates difficulties for management but is in the long run ineffective for the workers. For the heart of the problem lies at the work place, and must be dealt with in terms of organization and the relation of the worker to his work. It is beyond the reach of external "political" solutions, whether governmental or union. The problem was largely created by business management, and only business management can solve it.

We need a science of management that will recognize that the nature of human organization cannot be apprehended in terms of authoritarian concepts. We need to acknowledge that the purpose of a human organization, whether business or otherwise, can only be defined in terms of the people in it, flesh and blood men and women, with sentiments, ambitions, and needs of their own which range far beyond the confines of the organization. For the extent to which they serve the needs of the organization willingly and enthusiastically depends in the end upon the extent to which the organization serves their needs as sentient, aspiring human beings.

The growth and wide popularity of the science of human relations is encouraging. It represents an effort on management's part to secure a better understanding of what is going on within its organization and to develop higher orders of skill for dealing with its immediate and long-range problems. But even this hopeful development has its pitfalls. There is a danger that human relations will degenerate into a sort of "be nice to the guy" school of thought. Being "nice" to people is all well and good, but it is not enough. Sometimes management has to do things that are painful to people, and if its only hold on them consists in having been "nice," it will not retain their loyalty or support for long. Under such circumstances, people are likely to look around for someone else who promises to be "nicer." This "be nice to people" version of human relations is brittle; it will not stand up against a blow of any real severity.

Any realistic science or philosophy of management must be tough-minded. There is a place in it for sentiment but not for sentimentality. It must be founded on fundamental Christian ideals, but like Christianity itself, it must not mistake the easy life for the good life, nor sentiment for wisdom.

III

The challenge we are facing is no less than the preservation of all the things we value highest as Americans. If we can meet this challenge successfully, if we can develop ways and means for applying our democratic ideals more effectively within business itself, we will not only preserve our system but we can confidently expect a release of creative and productive energies as great as those released by the rise of the democratic states during the eighteenth and nineteenth centuries.

Industrial experience can stimulate the development of human potentials—or it can stultify growth and stifle the human spirit. Industrial organization can enrich and embellish individuality—or it can degrade men and women to dull and common levels of mediocrity. Industrial practice can strengthen the underpinnings of democracy—or it can riddle them to a hollow shell. The choice is management's. For on business leadership depends our ability to work out, in practical, realistic terms, the means for making *industrial* society the *good* society.

Chapter FIVE

Trends in Modern Management

The emergence of large-scale organization has had far-reaching effects not only on the external relations of business but on its internal workings as well. The characteristic human organization of modern industry can be traced to the influence of the new scale of business enterprise, along with its by-product, the so-called "scientific management movement."

I

Spectacular as were the mechanical inventions which are usually identified as the basis for the industrial revolution, the social innovations which made the utilization of these inventions possible (and which in a real sense called them into being) were more spectacular still.

Improvement in transportation and communication created the technical circumstances and provided the impetus for a broad geographical division of labor. But to make this possible there had to be a supporting *functional* division of labor. Before large-scale industry could arise, new institutions had to take the place of the direct, personal relationships which had previously existed between the small-scale local enterprise and its suppliers and customers. When raw materials began to be drawn from wider and wider areas and finished products began to be disposed of at greater and greater distances, jobbing and related functions had to be developed to perform the necessary tasks of mediation. As new and vastly more expensive equipment replaced the simpler tools and facilities of an earlier day, more adequate institutions for the mobilization of capital were required. As channels of distribution grew more attenuated, and larger resources were tied up in inventories awaiting sale and accounts receivable awaiting payment, better credit facilities became essential. These and other developments in the field of social organization were necessary to the rise of large-scale industry.

But equally revolutionary changes were required in the internal organization of the enterprise. The power loom could not be utilized in the home, nor the steam engine in the handicraft shop. Before the advantages of the Bessemer process could be realized, vast changes were necessary in the internal economy of the steel plant. Much more was involved than mere increase in scale of operation; the growth of new and specialized activities paralleled (but in complexity greatly exceeded) the trend toward geographical and functional specialization in the economy at large.

The creators of these new patterns of organization were largely the businessmen. It was they who saw the potentialities of the new mechanical inventions; it was they who worked out the social and economic arrangements that made it possible to use them; it was they who created the new patterns of production and distribution and devised the new systems of internal organization. The modern enterprise, except in rare cases, was not the old handicraft shop grown large; primarily, modern industry arose in response to myriad acts of creation by the entrepreneurs.

In part, the marked increase in specialization of work was a result of the scarcity of labor. The concentration of industry and the growth of establishments serving wide market areas increased the demand for labor vastly beyond the supply of skilled workers available or the ability of traditional apprentice methods to train. This scarcity encouraged the breaking down of complex skills into their simpler elements so that they could be learned more quickly by the inexperienced and unskilled workers industry found it necessary to employ. It was thus possible to make better use of the limited supply of technically trained people; such people could be "spread thinner," their skills made to "go further"—a process we have seen applied on a more deliberate and far-reaching scale in meeting the labor shortages of two world wars. The scarcity of labor also directed inventive efforts toward creating labor-saving (or rather, labor-extending) machinery, a task stimulated and made easier by the division of work into more and more elementary processes.

From the standpoint of management, these developments created crucial problems of control and coordination. Under previous systems of production, workers had produced whole (or reasonably whole) *products;* under the new system, they performed only *processes*. The productive unit was no longer the individual worker but the work group. More and more, as specialization and division of labor proceeded, the factory as a whole became the productive unit, a unit consisting perhaps of hundreds of operations each performed by a single operator, no one of whom could have turned out a complete product. The diverse activities of many different people had to be integrated into a new productive pattern. It was out of this need that management, as we know it today, emerged.

II

Frederick W. Taylor (1856–1915) was one of the earliest and most creative of those concerned with thinking through these problems of organization and control. In his efforts to bring some greater sense of order out of the chaos in the industry of his day he developed the concepts which were to form the basis of "scientific management."

Taylor's work produced remarkably fruitful results. These included the improvement of machinery and tools, the re-arrangement of equipment to facilitate flow of work, the improvement of material handling, the standardization of raw materials, the detailed analysis of production processes to eliminate unnecessary effort, and the development of new and better methods for record-keeping and control. Above all, he emphasized the importance of the proper planning of the entire production process to the end that raw materials and semi-finished parts should move through the shop by the shortest possible routes and on schedules that would insure the precise meeting, at every stage of production, of the necessary materials, tools, machines, and workmen. As a result of these efforts, Taylor went a long way toward bringing production out of the confusion in which he found it, and in doing so laid the foundations for a phenomenal increase in the productivity of American industry.

In the course of making these improvements, Taylor sought to apply to the problems of people working together the same concepts and methods he found so successful when applied to the problems of technical organization. Taylor was an engineer, and sought quite explicitly to set up organizations in the same manner he might design a machine. And he visualized the role of people within the organization in precisely the same manner as he visualized the component parts of a mechanism.

"A complicated and delicately adjusted machine" was a favorite figure of speech.

The entrepreneur had already learned to rely heavily on the engineer in carrying out his plans. The engineer was indispensable in building the railroads, the bridges, the factories, the machines—the visible elements of the new economic organization being put together by the entrepreneur. It was natural, then, that the entrepreneur should also look to the engineer to work out problems of internal organization, of work flow and work processes, of division of labor within the plant—for these were "details" largely beyond the range of interest of the entrepreneur concerned with putting together the major elements of the emerging industrial pattern. For their own part, the engineers found it necessary to interest themselves in problems of organization and management: they had invented and designed the new machinery of production and they soon found that their machines would work but poorly unless properly served by the human components of the organization. It is no accident that the engineers formed the first occupational group in our society to interest itself actively in problems of management per se, nor that the American Society of Mechanical Engineers became the principal forum of the scientific management movement.

The engineers have strongly influenced our thinking about problems of organization and human relations. If we consider closely our generally accepted theories of organization, we cannot help but note the parallel to machine theory. Our ideal of an effective organization has been a "smoothly running machine," an organization in which all parts function with a minimum of friction and a maximum economy of effort. Each component is seen as carefully designed for its particular task, and the whole as responding automatically to the touch of the operator's hand. Our very phraseology employs mechanical images. Organization charts are frequently referred to as "blueprints." "Management engineering" and "human engineering" have become recognized occupations. All our thinking about organization displays a strongly mechanical turn of mind.

Unfortunately for the course of industry, the methods and concepts of engineering have proved inappropriate to human organization; the engineering mode of thought has distorted the perceptions of the scientific managers and seriously misdirected their efforts. Particularly unfortunate has been the effort to force man to adapt to the technical organization rather than seeking ways to adapt the technical organization to man.

III

It was the constant effort of the scientific managers—chiefly through detailed job study and time and motion analysis—to break jobs down into increasingly smaller parcels, with specific, detailed instructions as to exactly what the worker should do and how he should do it. A consequence of this was a drastic re-division of functions between management and workers in which the creative, thinking aspects of work were reserved to management. Taylor was quite explicit in this: "All possible brain work should be removed from the shop and centered in the planning and laying out department."[1] Thus jobs that were already becoming machine-like through progressive physical simplification became even more so through the deliberate effort to minimize the characteristics of workers that most significantly differentiate them from machines.

The principle of specialization was not confined to workers at the machine or bench but was extended to management as well. By his sweeping redivision of labor as between workers

[1] Frederick W. Taylor, *Scientific Management* (New York: Harper & Brothers, 1947), pp. 98–99.

and management, Taylor so increased the burden on management that a considerable further division of labor within management became essential. Just as Taylor sought to simplify operators' jobs so that they could be performed by less skilled people, so he sought to break management down into its component parts so that they too would be within the capacities of those available for managerial assignments. Thus "each man from the assistant superintendent down shall have as few functions as possible to perform. If practicable the work of each man in the management should be confined to the performance of a single leading function."[2] It was Taylor's thought that each of these specialized people in management should exercise direct supervision over the work force with respect to their particular specialty. This, however, proved cumbersome because workers received orders and instructions —frequently conflicting—from too many people. Those coming after Taylor preserved the idea of specialization within management but developed the "line and staff" concept whereby direct supervision of workers was reserved to the line and the various specializations organized into staffs advisory or supplementary to the line. Thus the principle of managerial specialization was consolidated.

The same logic encouraged departmental specialization. Through the application of this principle, which for convenience may be referred to as "functionalization," various activities within organizations were grouped together not in terms of the purposes they were intended to serve but in terms of their technical similarity to each other. Thus, factories which had previously been organized on the basis of products were reorganized in such a way as to bring together in one department all lathes, in another department all drill presses, in another department all milling machines, etc. (the "process

[2] Taylor, *op. cit.*, p. 99.

shop" vs. the "product shop"). In department stores the basic function of buying and selling merchandise was broken down into a "merchandising function" concerned with buying, advertising, and displaying goods, and an "operating function" concerned with receiving, warehousing, selling, and delivering goods. Throughout, the theory was that grouping activities on the basis of their technical similarity rather than on the basis of the purposes they served would permit better supervision, increase flexibility, smooth out peaks and valleys in work load, and generally improve efficiency.

The significant feature of this process of individual and departmental specialization was not so much that it made possible the use of "cheaper men" (Taylor's phrase) nor that it represented, as has often been alleged, a wholesale "deskilling" of work. Workers who were already skilled—and thereby relatively high-priced—were not, by and large, forced back to the ranks of the semiskilled and the unskilled. Typically, they moved into supervisory and management positions where their ability and experience—above all, their knowledge of what production actually required—were urgently needed. Moreover many newcomers to industrial life, who were without skill and who otherwise would have been condemned to a life of common labor, had an opportunity to move into at least semiskilled work.

There are other grounds, however, on which the system of work specialization was open to serious criticism: It failed to make proper use of industry's human resources; it relieved workers of initiative and responsibility; and it created needlessly complex organizational structures which vastly increased the problems of coordination and control.

The gravest weakness was the failure to recognize and utilize properly management's most valuable resource: the complex and multiple capacities of people. On the contrary, the scientific managers deliberately sought to utilize as narrow a band of personality and as narrow a range of ability as ingenuity could devise. The process has been fantastically wasteful for industry and society.

The difficulty is greatly increased when not only individual operations but the work of entire departments is specialized— the functional type of organization. One consequence of functionalization, when carried to the extremes encouraged by scientific management theory, is its tendency to enforce the conception of people as *means*. On the one hand, the tendency toward over-functionalization arises from this type of conception; on the other hand, over-functionalization, once established, makes it impossible to deal with people on any other basis. Individual activities no longer have meaning or significance in themselves, and those who perform them have no value except as means for helping to accomplish the broader, over-all tasks to which the whole organization is devoted.

Over-functionalization makes more general and more acute one of the common errors of our times—the error of dealing with people by categories of status and function rather than as individuals. Despite the frequent protestations of management today about the importance of the individual, over-functionalization makes it difficult, and often impossible, to deal with people on individual terms.

A second weakness was the extent to which initiative and responsibility were transferred from workers to management. In part, this was an inevitable consequence of destroying the meaning of work itself. Because jobs had little meaning for their own sake, workers were likely to have little feeling of responsibility for them. But to this natural result of obscuring the workers' relation to the whole was added another and more potent influence: their deliberate exclusion from the exercise of initiative.

Taylor emphasized the importance, under his system, of "the intimate cooperation of the management with the workmen, so that together they do the work in accordance with the scientific laws that have been developed."[3] But as workers had no part in the determination and interpretation of these "laws," this kind of cooperation consisted simply of, "You do what I tell you to do"; not cooperation but docility was called for. As Taylor himself often admonished workers, "You are not supposed to think. There are other people paid for thinking around here."[4] In statements of this kind, Taylor revealed his basic attitudes toward workers. He frequently referred to them as children and often used schoolroom analogies. Looking on workers as essentially dependent and immature—to be enticed by rewards and threatened by punishments—it is understandable that Taylor had difficulty seeing them as interested in taking an adult attitude toward their work and capable of making an adult contribution to it.

Management today is seriously concerned with what it considers the apathy of workers, their lack of concern for efficiency, their indifference to finding new and better ways of doing their jobs. Much of the difficulty lies in the fact that industry, following the tenets of scientific management, has systematically deprived workers of real and effective participation in industry. Industry is reaping what it has sown, for without participation there can be neither initiative nor responsibility.

By minutely subdividing operations, by separating the "thinking" parts of work from the "doing," by increasing specialization within management itself, and by grouping activities on the basis of specialized functions, scientific management enormously complicated the problems of coordination and control. This was the third major weakness of the system of specialization developed under Taylor's influence.

[3] Taylor, *op. cit.* p. 115.
[4] Frank Barkley Copley, *Frederick W. Taylor, Father of Scientific Management* (New York: Harper & Brothers, 1923), vol. I, p. 189.

Integration was conceived by Taylor as a purely mechanical process to be achieved by purely mechanical means. The
organization was set up like a machine and it had to be
operated like a machine. But because its components were
human rather than mechanical, the task of controlling and
directing it taxed the ingenuity of the scientific managers. The
elaborate contrivances of the modern industrial organization,
the masses of paper work and red tape, the layers on layers of
supervision, the luxuriant growth of staff—all these are evidence of the difficulty of controlling human organizations in
terms of mechanistic principles.

The sole purpose of setting up functional units is to enable
each to achieve a more efficient system. Each unit, therefore,
tends to operate primarily in terms of its own logics, that is,
the needs of its own system and technology. Because the technical requirements of efficiency are likely to be different for
each function (else why set them up as separate divisions?)
the logics of each are likely to vary accordingly. And because
each function is only part of the whole, the logics of each function will tend to differ from the logics of the whole. To the
extent that they differ, and they often differ greatly, there is
likely to be conflict.

It is a commonplace that economic interests influence attitudes, as witness the frequently conflicting points of view of
farmers, importers, and manufacturers. It is not so generally
recognized that functional interests within an organization
likewise influence attitudes. To some extent this is a matter of
perspective. Those looking at an organization from different
angles of vision are likely to see the same things somewhat differently. One of the consequences of over-functionalization
has been the splitting up of organizations into many distinct
subgroups, each with a somewhat different point of view, each
with a somewhat different set of attitudes and interests, and
each in some degree of conflict with the others. Over-function-

alization thus vastly increases and complicates the task of integrating and unifying the organization as a whole.

As the supervisory hierarchy becomes extended, management finds it necessary to institute more and more formal controls. These may be more or less complex, depending on the particular technologies involved. In the functional type of organization, however, all of them are likely to be characterized by a considerable degree of abstractness. The effectiveness of the organization as a whole may be judged in terms of physical output, or volume of sales, or the profit and loss statement. But where the internal structure of the organization is broken down into a series of functional divisions, there are no "natural" standards of performance and management is forced to exercise considerable ingenuity in inventing controls which it can use for administrative purposes. Unfortunately, contrived controls such as these, far from facilitating interdivisional cooperation, often become themselves a source of conflict. The individual supervisor or executive is under compulsion to operate in such a manner as to make a good showing in terms of the particular set of controls to which he is subject, and often he can do so only at the expense of effective collaboration across divisional lines.

Taylor often noted that modern industry requires intimate cooperation; but he overlooked the fact that cooperation must be between *real people,* not between abstract functions. "Real people" were lost in the intricacies of his system. As he himself was fond of saying: "In the past the man has been first; in the future the system must be first."[5] By his reliance on strictly mechanical forms of integration he stultified the natural tendencies of people working together to achieve a more organic form of integration, and thus increased still further his dependence on mechanical contrivances.

Scientific management stressed the rational approach, the

5 Taylor, *op. cit.,* p. 7.

careful and deliberate fashioning of means to ends. The danger of such an approach lies in the fact that means may be too narrowly designed for overly restricted ends and that the very precision of the means-ends calculus is bound to impair flexibility and adaptability.

IV

Taylor's personality emerges with great clarity from his writings. His virtual obsession to control the environment around him was expressed in everything he did: in his home life, his gardening, his golfing; even his afternoon stroll was not a casual affair but something to be carefully planned and rigidly followed. Nothing was left to chance if in any way chance could be avoided. Every personal action was thought through carefully, all contingencies considered, and steps taken to guard against extraneous developments. And when, despite all precautions, something did occur to upset his plans he gave evidence of great internal distress—distress that sometimes expressed itself in blazing anger and sometimes in black brooding.

Taylor's theories of management bear the unmistakable impress of this characteristic. His biographer thus states the relation between his system and his temperament:

Just as he strove to intellectualize himself—that is, manage his whole life according to reason, right arrangement, and systematic regulation—so he sought to intellectualize industrial management. In each case the central idea was the same—*control!* First we see the intellect using its powers of analysis, abstraction, and comparison for the setting up of definite standards. No sooner is this done than all things seem to conspire to break down the standards. And in one's power to resist this conspiracy lies one's control.[6]

[6] Copley, *op. cit.*, vol. I, p. 350.

From his writings and his biography one gets the impression of a rigid, insecure personality, desperately afraid of the unknown and the unforeseen, able to face the world with reasonable equanimity only if everything possible has been done to keep the world in its place and to guard against anything that might upset his careful, painstaking plans. Taylor presented to the world a well-organized, well-adjusted front, and probably even his closest friends and associates were unaware, or only dimly aware, of this deeper side of his temperament. But his personal organization and adjustment consisted precisely in the extent to which he had developed his skill of control. Looking on the world in this way, distrusting it, fearful of anything he had not anticipated and planned for, it is clear why he left so little room in his system for initiative and spontaneity on the part of workers—or even, for that matter, on the part of managers.

Reference has been made to the shortcomings of Taylor's work which seem to relate to the fact that he was an engineer. Perhaps the deeper truth is that his temperament and character predisposed him to an unduly narrow engineering approach, and that he found the mechanistic concepts of engineering admirably adapted to the needs of his personality. Perhaps a more adequate personality would have been able to use the engineering concepts more constructively, to adapt them more effectively to the special characteristics and potentialities of human organization, and to have set the whole future course of management along more positive, more creative lines.

V

The full implications of the obsession for control in the scientific management movement became even more apparent in Taylor's followers. It was all very well, these men found, to organize the work of the shop, but no sooner was everything under control there than influences from outside the shop, from other segments of the enterprise (e.g., sales, finance), began to impinge upon and upset their neatly contrived arrangements. Thus the scientific managers soon began to be concerned with the necessity for extending their control to the entire enterprise. But this, too, proved insufficient, for there were external pressures on the enterprise itself that had to be organized and controlled before scientific management could come into its own.

There is significance, therefore, in the fairly general tendency among scientific managers to move from planning and control within the individual plant to thinking in terms of a "planned society." As one of them put it, "Taylor's revolution in mental attitude, to be effective, cannot stop short of the organized community."[7] Henry L. Gantt, one of the most distinguished of Taylor's followers, railed against "commercial men" and financiers and demanded that the control of industry—all industry—be turned over to the engineers who alone knew how to run "the huge and delicate apparatus."[8] "Most assuredly," he asserted, "finance and industry must be socialized somehow."[9] He was in favor of an organization "similar to the cartel system," wherein prices would be fixed by committees of producers, distributors, and consumers; reason, planning, and control were to replace the chaotic economic processes he saw about him.[10]

In 1916 Gantt proposed a fantastic organization, called "The New Machine," which was to be "a conspiracy [*sic!*] of men of science, engineers, chemists, land and sea tamers and general masters of arts and materials—a fellowship at deadly

[7] Robert Bruere, "Industrial Relations," from *Scientific Management* (New York: Harper & Brothers, 1947), p. 464.

[8] Leon Pratt Alford, *Henry Lawrence Gantt* (New York: Harper & Brothers, 1934), p. 273.

[9] *Ibid.*, p. 265.

[10] *Ibid.*, p. 298.

enmity with all parasites and pretenders—held together in their war against humbugs by their common love of what is really so and by their common scorn of purse-lipped, pious altruisms."[11] The aim of the New Machine, which was clearly a forerunner of Technocracy, was apparently some form of corporate state, dimly foreseen, whose economic system would consist largely of public service corporations—managed, of course, by engineers trained in the skills of scientific management.

Scientific management has been taken up enthusiastically in Europe where it has had perhaps an even wider vogue than in this country. Its most marked expression has been the rationalization movement, which emphasized the "planning" element of scientific management to a far greater degree than the American variety. "Planning" has for long been very much in the spirit of European business, as witness the strength of the cartel system. The importation of scientific management from America has merely reinforced the trend.

But it is in Soviet Russia that scientific management has had its fullest flowering. Lenin looked on the Taylor system as the "last word in capitalism" and encouraged its "systematic trial and adoption" in Russia as a means for accelerating industrial production. The Stakhanovist movement has many features in common with American techniques of motion study. And Russia's planning has been characterized as "an attempt to do on a national scale what scientific management was doing within the individual plant."[12] The author of this statement, a contemporary student of scientific management, makes the following interesting comment:

Another feature of the Russian situation that is different from that in American management is that scientific management (ra-

---

[11] *Ibid.*, p. 265. See pp. 264–77 for an account of "The New Machine."
[12] George Filipetti, *Industrial Management in Transition,* (Chicago, Richard D. Irwin, Inc., 1949), p. 9.

tionalization) has become a mass movement. In most of the other countries, and particularly in the United States, it has been a matter determined by individual plant managements. Progress has been made in a more or less informal or hit-or-miss fashion, with plants gradually adopting such techniques as the management may be familiar with or which appear to be applicable. As a result the extension of techniques and principles has been very irregular and not widely understood. Certainly they are not now fully employed nor fully understood in Russia, but the development of a national program along these lines gives promise of effecting some startling results.[13]

Note the suggestion of envy at the lack of equal authority in this country to extend the scope of scientific management. Note, too, the implied deprecation of a system which allows each individual management to choose which if any elements of scientific management it will adopt. "Just think," he seems to be saying, "what startling results we would have in *this* country if only the scientific managers had authority to force management to see the light and follow their better principles."

There are interesting parallels between communism and scientific management. In both cases workers are seen as means rather than ends, doers rather than planners or initiators; to be manipulated—by persuasion if possible, by coercion if necessary—in other interests and for other needs than their own.

In any event, the "planning" penchant of scientific management, as it was implicit in Taylor's work and as it has been explicit from Gantt down, is worth noting. Today, the word "planning" (in the sense of government intervention and control) carries an evil connotation in this country—particularly in management circles—it did not carry in like degree a generation ago. Especially during the Great Depression "planning" had a vogue which it has since lost. But the tendency

[13] *Ibid.,* pp. 202–203.

toward what in an earlier day was frankly called "planning" is nonetheless still present in modern writings on scientific management. And it is a tendency which will continue to be inherent in the movement so long as its major emphasis is on *control*.

The obsession for control springs from the failure to recognize or appreciate the value of spontaneity, either in everyday work or in economic processes. Hence the need for *planning*. Hence the machine as the idea for human organization. For the machine has no will of its own. Its parts have no urge to independent action. Thinking, direction—even purpose— must be provided from outside or above. To those who have inherited Taylor's point of view, "human nature" is something annoying—unavoidable, perhaps, but regrettably so, and to be kept in bounds so far as possible.

From distrust of spontaneity in the work place it is a short step to distrust of spontaneity in the market place. Today it is unfashionable to speak of planning outside the particular enterprise—for that involves government, and all "right-minded people" want less, not more, government interference in economic affairs. But let there be a serious downturn in business, let the present smooth functioning of markets collapse under the blows of economic adversity, and the habit of mind that thinks in terms of mechanistic organization of the enterprise will make it easy to think in terms of mechanistic organization of the economy.

The Dynamics of Organization Structure

In the literature of scientific management, organization structure is dealt with essentially as a technical problem: the orderly and logical arrangement of specialized functions into an over-all productive pattern. What the scientific managers failed to apprehend is that organization structure has a profound influence on the people who comprise the organization, the character of the relations which grow up between them, and the quality of the experience they derive as participants in the productive process.

I

One of the earliest findings of human relations research was that the manner in which people relate themselves to each other in the performance of their work is often considerably at variance with the pattern of relationships seemingly prescribed by the formal organization. In recognition of this phenomenon, Elton Mayo developed the concept of "informal organization." The formal organization is simply the manner in which management structures the relationships between functions and activities, and is commonly expressed in the form of an organization chart. The informal organization is the pattern of personal relationships developed by the spontaneous interaction of members of the work force. Informal groups owe their cohesiveness, which is often great, to interests their members hold in common: e.g., working together in close proximity, exposure to pressures from other groups or from management, age and length of service, and so forth. A considerable literature has emerged on the manner in which the informal organization influences and often greatly distorts the formal, in the sense that the organization actually works quite differently from the way it is "supposed" to work. Little attention, however, has been given to the converse, the way in which the formal organization influences and shapes the informal organization.

The formal organization may be considered as the broad outline of division of labor within the enterprise or plant. It prescribes the flow of work, the major responsibilities of each operating unit, and the chain of command. The informal organization does not develop in a vacuum but within the structure of the formal. Because the formal organization largely determines which groups will interact with which, what kinds of technical relationships will obtain within and between groups, and what kinds of interests different categories of workers will have in common, it largely determines the composition of the informal groups and profoundly influences their behavior.

Organizations can be set up in such a way as to foster the patterning of personal relations around the task of getting the work done or around the goal of resisting supervisory pressure. This is another way of saying that the formal organization encourages the development of informal groups which either support the aims of the formal organization or are in conflict with those aims. The functional type of organization tends to create informal groups of the latter variety.

This is illustrated in the experience of a large midwestern factory which utilized a limited number of manufacturing processes to turn out a variety of end products. Originally, this plant was organized on a process basis whereby similar activities and machines (lathes, punch presses, milling, assembly, etc.) were grouped in separate departments. Products in course of manufacture moved from one department to the next, workers in each department performing in sequence the prescribed mechanical operations. There were also service departments (e.g., inspection and methods), each reporting up a separate chain of command and each with its own supervisory hierarchy. Conflicts between processing and service departments were frequent and considered more or less normal.

Under the influence of this organization structure, informal groups tended to organize along departmental lines. Thus, to the operators in the processing departments, inspectors and methods men were enemies, and cooperating to keep these "outsiders" from constituting too great a threat was an inevitable result—in the minds of the workers a wholly legitimate form of self-protection. For their part, inspectors and methods men tended to look on the operators as threats to themselves, and their own informal groups were oriented accordingly.

There was also frequent conflict among the processing departments over schedules and quality of work. Here again workers tended to coalesce informally along departmental lines to resist external criticisms and pressures. Much of the time of the higher levels of plant supervision was spent in coordinating the activities of departments, settling differences, and otherwise striving to maintain a smooth flow of operations. Extensive paper work and record keeping was necessary to keep track of materials and of work at various stages of processing, and to provide those at higher levels with the information and controls they needed to keep the work of the plant properly meshed together.

Because of difficulties such as these, the plant was eventually reorganized on a product rather than a process basis. Each department became responsible for turning out a completed product, and was furnished with all the machines, facilities, and job skills necessary for that purpose. The separate inspection and methods departments were broken up and their personnel assigned to the various product departments, responsible directly to the individual department heads.

This change in formal organization induced a substantial change in the pattern and quality of worker and group relationships. Inspectors ceased to be a threat to the operators. They were still concerned with quality of output; but now that they were an integral part of a departmental work group their role became that of working *with* rather than *against* the operators to maintain quality. The role of the methods men became that of helping to find easier and more efficient ways of getting work done. Men operating different types of machines developed a new relationship with each other. When an operator on one machine fell behind schedule or ran into other difficulties, he would get help from operators of other machines, or they would adjust their own work pace until the problem was resolved.

There was still as much *individual* job specialization as there had been before, but now that the specialized operations were organized around the task of turning out finished products the relationships between jobs and between the men performing them became quite different. Jobs acquired a meaning they had not had before. The lathe operator was not merely turning a piece of metal, the punch press operator was not merely punching out shapes, the drill press operator was not merely drilling holes. Inspection was no longer catching a worker trying to pass off shoddy work. Each of these tasks now made sense because it was part of a whole that could be readily seen and appreciated, not only by those performing each particular task but by those around them performing other tasks.

A further important consequence of the shift from a process to a product type of organization was a considerable simplification of the supervisory hierarchy, a substantial reduction in paper work, and the elimination of many hitherto essential formal and systematic controls. Output could be maintained with less close and detailed supervision because there was an apprehendable relation between individual effort and group result. Coordination of functions was accomplished more informally and less through deliberate supervisory action; employees on different but dovetailing operations worked things out together without having to go through a series of organizational channels. Teamwork was better, not because management preached it, but because the structure of the organization raised fewer impediments to the kind of cooperation that is likely to develop spontaneously among adult men and women if it has a chance.

A particularly significant aspect of the change in the structure of the formal organization was its impact on the informal. Reflecting the new patterns of interpersonal relations created by the new patterns of formal job relations, the informal groups gradually began to shift in composition and orientation. Psychic and physical energies that had once been dissipated in friction came to be devoted to productive purposes, with benefits not only to the enterprise but to the workers as well. The aims of the informal and the formal organizations did not, of course, become identical, but there was a substantially greater degree of identity than had previously prevailed.

II

Human relations research has made much of the fact that the sentiments and values of small work groups are frequently at variance with those of management. Before drawing any sweeping conclusions from the evidence so far at hand, it might be well to review that evidence in the light of the kinds of organization structures within which small work groups develop. It is a reasonable speculation that such a review would indicate that where the formal organization is built around technical processes or abstract functions, as in the functional form of organization, informal groups will tend to be oriented in opposition to management, but that this is much less likely to be the case where the formal structure is so arranged as to bring together in close physical proximity and intimate organizational unity all the operations or processes needed to produce a meaningful end product.

The small work group has great cohesiveness and power, which are often used in ways antagonistic to management. But this does not mean that the aims and values of the small work group are always and necessarily anti-management. Management has it within its power to create circumstances in which the orientation of the small work group can more nearly parallel the orientation of management. Organization structure is certainly not the only factor, but it has a powerful influence. A useful test of organizational effectiveness might well be the extent to which the aims and sentiments of the formal and informal organizations tend to conflict or coincide. Measures for this purpose, if properly worked out, might be much more useful in diagnosing problems of management-employee relations than the more familiar morale survey.

The influence of structure on patterns of personal relationship and organizational effectiveness may be observed in many different contexts. British coal mines are certainly not examples of efficient production or of good management-employee relations. And yet the bad can be made worse, as one British mine found. Apparently in an effort to apply some of the principles of scientific management, mining operations which had formerly been handled by small groups of miners and completed on the same shift were rearranged in a series of successive operations spread out over a three-shift, twenty-four-hour cycle. Output fell sharply. No single group of workers felt responsible for the process as a whole, and there was constant friction between shifts. A change in the structure of the formal organization thus made conflict with the informal inevitable.[1]

The experience of a California hospital for retarded children illustrates the converse of this principle. In this institution half the patients were kept strapped to their cribs to keep them from hurting themselves. Older patients who were able to do simple chores aided in the care of the more helpless. Their work was organized on an assembly-line basis: some did nothing but scrub floors, others nothing but change diapers, others nothing but feeding. A new psychiatric technician, placed in charge of a cottage housing a hundred youngsters, changed all this. She unchained the children, she abolished the assembly line, and she put each helper in charge of three children with responsibility for doing all that was necessary for their care. "That's the way it's done in families," she said.

[1] Leonard R. Sayles, "Work Behavior and the Larger Organization," *Research in Industrial Human Relations* (New York: Harper & Brothers, 1957), p. 137.

"You don't have one person just washing diapers, another feeding the baby."[2]

This change in organization altered the entire atmosphere of the cottage and the people in it. The helpers began to take more interest in their jobs and in their charges. A sense of pride and of personal responsibility developed. And the younger, more helpless patients responded also, not only to the greater freedom they were allowed but to the warmer, more sympathetic, more human relationships that grew between themselves and the older helpers to whose care they were committed. There is a simple but deeply significant lesson here for all who are concerned with the problems of how people live and work together.

Many thoughtful observers of modern society are deeply concerned with the loss of local autonomy and the centralization of power which have attended the growth of giant organizations in government, business, and labor. These are realistic apprehensions. The esteem in which small groups, small communities, small businesses are generally held has solid foundations. For example, work experience in smaller organizational units seems to be more stimulating and more rewarding than work experience in larger units.

The reasons for this are fairly clear. Employees in smaller units have a much better opportunity to know each other, so that cooperation between individuals and departments can develop on a more personal, informal basis and not be so largely dependent on impersonal systems and administrative controls. In a large mail order plant, for instance, those who do the detailed work of controlling an inventory of tens of thousands of items and those who actually handle the merchandise itself must work in close coordination with each other; but because of the large number of people in each

[2] *Time* magazine, March 3, 1952.

group, personal relations across divisional lines are few and coordination between the separate but related functions must be accomplished through a complex system of procedures. In a small retail store, where there must likewise be coordination between such functions as inventory control and the handling of merchandise, the situation is quite different. Salespeople, office clerks, and those in the receiving and shipping rooms know each other on a first-name basis and cooperation between them is a personal matter. Cooperation develops spontaneously and not as a result of orders or of a system of formal procedures set up to establish coordination. An organization such as this operates primarily through the face-to-face relationships of its members and only secondarily through impersonal, institutionalized relationships.

In the smaller organization, employees see much more readily where they themselves "fit" into the organization and the significance of their jobs in the whole scheme of things. In fact, seeing where they "fit" is an important part of being able to cooperate. In large, complex organizations, cooperation must depend to a much greater extent on a status system (expressed in an appropriate system of status symbols), which defines working relationships in more or less purely technical terms. The record clerk in a mail order plant has difficulty seeing beyond her routine task of processing inventory control cards; stockmen and order fillers are a world apart. The girl in the office of a small store can readily see the relationship between her work and that of other employees, and the manner in which all their efforts dovetail into the over-all task of serving the customer.

In particular, the relationship between the job and the customer is more readily apparent in the smaller retail store than in the large mail order plant. To mail order employees, the merchandise they handle is so many packages, so many pounds, so many hours of labor. The management of the mail order plant is concerned with filling orders promptly and getting the merchandise into the customers' hands on schedule, but its interest, too, is abstract: the goods is so many dollars, not a doll buggy or a dress or an electric drill for a flesh and blood human being. Jobs in smaller units, in other words, are likely to have greater personal significance than is possible in larger units simply because, in the former, the relationship to something which transcends the job itself is much more readily apparent. This is true not only in merchandising organizations but in other types as well.

A further advantage of smaller organizations lies in the fact that closer contacts between the executives and rank and file tend to result in friendlier, easier relationships. To employees in such units, the "big boss" is not some remote, little-known, semimythical personage but an individual to be liked or disliked on a basis of personal acquaintance. In large organizations, myths about "those guys in the front office" are often the chief means by which rank-and-file employees arrive at their feelings toward those in higher levels of management. These myths often represent badly distorted images of the individuals in question, distortions which could be readily corrected if the organization were small enough to provide opportunity for more frequent personal contact.

More frequent, more personal contact between executives and rank and file makes possible a much better understanding of one another's problems and points of view and greatly facilitates the adjustment of difficulties which may arise. In larger and more complex organizations action not only tends to be delayed but may not really compose the difficulty because the person making the controlling decision is so far removed from the scene that he receives a garbled version of the problem and the real issue.

In sum, the smaller organization represents a simpler social system. There are fewer people, fewer levels in the organizational hierarchy, and a less minute subdivision of labor. It is easier for the employee to adapt himself to such a system and to win a place in it. His work becomes more meaningful, both to him and to his associates, because he and they can readily see its relation and importance to other functions and to the organization as a whole. The organization operates primarily through the face-to-face relationships of its members and only secondarily through impersonal, institutionalized relationships. The closer relations between the individual employee and higher executives in such a situation is only one aspect—but an important one—of the relatively simple and integrated social system of the smaller organization.

III

Modern industrial society faces a serious dilemma: on the one hand, the tendency of technological change to foster the growth of large organizations and, on the other, the evil consequences attendant on such growth. But the dilemma is more apparent than real, for there is no inherent reason why it should not be possible to break down even the largest organization into a series of relatively small components, each of which can enjoy a large measure of local autonomy and each of which can function as and exhibit the charactertistics of a small organization. Effective internal decentralization can make large organizations at once more efficient technically and more democratic socially. It should also make them more adaptive and give them incomparably greater survival power.

The breaking down of larger organizations into smaller units must be done in such a manner as to permit these smaller units to function as integrated and meaningful entities. This will require the scrapping or the substantial modification of the concept of functional organization. For *functionalization has the inevitable effect of increasing the size of the adminis-*

*trative unit and making effective decentralization impossible
beyond the point in the organization structure where the process of functionalization begins.*

This fact can be illustrated by a hypothetical example. Assume an organization that performs three primary functions
or operations, A, B, and C. Assume, further, that the volume
of output requires three units each of A, B, and C. Under
these circumstances, the organization could be set up in either
of two ways:

1. As three product divisions, with one unit of each function (A, B, and C) represented in each division. Such an
organization could be illustrated in this manner ("S" indicat-
ing first line supervision and "M" plant management):

$$
\begin{array}{ccc}
 & M & \\
S & S & S \\
A\ B\ C & A\ B\ C & A\ B\ C
\end{array}
$$

Fig. 1

2. As three functional divisions, one division having all
three A units, another all three B units, and the third all three
C units. Such an organization might be diagramed as follows:

$$
\begin{array}{ccc}
 & M & \\
S & S & S \\
A\ A\ A & B\ B\ B & C\ C\ C
\end{array}
$$

Fig. 2

Whatever other differences there might be in the way these two forms of operation work, the size of the administrative unit would be much greater in the second case than in the first. In the ABC or product-type structure illustrated in Figure 1, the administrative unit is the division, because each division, comprising as it does all activities essential to turning out a completed product, can operate with a high degree of autonomy. The total organization is composed of three relatively independent units, any of which could continue to function even if the others shut down (Fig. 3).

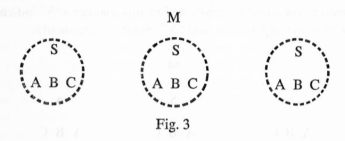

Fig. 3

In the AAA or functional type of organization, however, no division can operate except in the closest coordination with both the others; any difficulty in one will have immediate repercussions in the others, and if one breaks down the others must soon come to a halt. In this case, the administrative unit is no longer the division but must of necessity be the organization as a whole (Fig. 4). In the current example, this unit is by definition three times as large as that represented in Figure 3 and to that extent far more subject to the difficulties inherent in larger size per se.

The best definition of the size of the administrative unit is the extent to which responsibility and authority can be delegated down the line. *The administrative unit can be no smaller than that portion of the organization falling within the juris-*

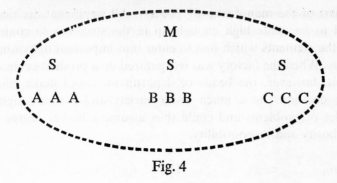

Fig. 4

diction of an individual who controls enough elements of the total process to make effective decisions regarding the total process. In the integrated type of organization represented by Figures 1 and 3, M, the plant manager, can delegate a substantial measure of authority and responsibility to each of his three S's, because each S has under his direct supervision and control all the functions necessary to turn out a completed product. In the functional type of organization represented by Figures 2 and 4, however, M can delegate only a limited amount of authority and responsibility. Each S supervises a single function and therefore controls only part of the total process. All significant decisions must be made by M; for only he holds within his hands all the elements which must be kept in proper balance. All that he can delegate effectively are such matters as pertain immediately and more or less exclusively to each of the individual functions, and in practice these are likely to be largely routine.

This was one of the problems of the process-centered organization of the midwestern factory previously described. Under this arrangement, the amount of authority and responsibility that higher management could delegate to the individual department heads was limited because each head supervised only a single function and therefore had effective control over only a part of the manufacturing process. All significant decisions had to be made high enough up in the structure to control all the elements which had to enter into important determinations. When the factory was reorganized on a product-centered basis, however, the heads of departments could make effective decisions on a much wider variety and a much higher order of problems and could thus assume a higher degree of authority and responsibility.

IV

The same point can be illustrated by reference to the parent buying organization of Sears, Roebuck and Co. which is widely known in management circles for the unusual extent to which authority and responsibility are delegated down the line. This delegation is an operative reality not only because higher management wishes it but because an organization structure has been created which makes it possible.

The Sears buying organization heads up to a merchandising vice president. Its primary functions are the procurement of merchandise sold through the company's retail stores and mail order plants, and the provision of over-all guidance to the sales promotional activities of the field. Buying activities are divided among forty buying departments, each headed by a supervisor who reports directly to the merchandising vice president. Also reporting to this officer are four staff assistants, each with an organizational unit appropriate to his special duties: an assistant on buying, a retail merchandise manager, a mail order merchandise manager, and a merchandise controller. These four executives serve in a "staff" capacity to the merchandising vice president, to form the "general merchandise office."

The organization of each buying department parallels that of the general merchandise office. Reporting to each supervisor is a retail sales manager, a mail order sales manager, a merchandise controller, and from five to twenty buyers depending on the volume and complexity of the merchandise line. As in the case of the parallel functions in the general merchandise office, the retail and mail order sales managers and the merchandise controllers serve the departmental supervisors and the buyers in a "staff" capacity. Each of these staff people also maintains close liaison with his parallel function at the general merchandise office level. The assistant on buying in the general merchandise office, in addition to serving the merchandising vice president, assists the buyers and supervisors in various ways, particularly with respect to long-range planning and development.

The structure of the parent merchandising organization is thus essentially quite simple. Each of the forty buying departments is held directly responsible for its own sales and profit results. The four basic functions necessary to achieve such results are an integral part of each buying department, and each of these functions is likewise represented in the general merchandise office, whence various essential services are available as needed. As the basic unit of the over-all merchandising organization is the buying department, so the basic unit of the buying department is the individual buyer, who is the focal point around which all other activities revolve.

By setting up the organization in this way, the various specialized and sometimes highly technical functions which must necessarily be performed are kept closely related to the central purposes to be served: the efficient buying of merchandise and the successful promotion of sales through the retail and mail order stores. In consequence of this arrangement, substantial authority and responsibility can be delegated by the general merchandise office not only to the supervisors of the buying departments but, through them, to the individual buyers as well.

This would not be the case if the parent merchandising organization were set up on a functional basis—if, for example, the work of the staff specialists in the various buying departments were pulled into their parallel functional units at the general merchandise office level, leaving only supervisors and buyers in the buying departments. On the surface there might seem to be a certain amount of logic in such a course. It might be argued that by means of such a regrouping it would be possible to eliminate a number of jobs, as for example through having one man handle the retail sales management of two or more smaller departments. It might be further argued that better supervision and coordination could be provided because the men performing each function would be working directly for the top man for that function (and hence the man presumably most skilled in it) rather than for the buying department supervisors who, whatever their skill in buying, might be wanting in some of the functional skills. And because of this closer and more "professional" supervision, it might also be possible to use people of somewhat lower caliber and hence less costly and more readily available.

Such an organization might be possible but the arguments for it are specious. For one thing, it would greatly complicate the formal organization structure and make far more difficult the intimate, informal collaboration within and across departmental lines that is so striking a feature of the present system. To take the place of that informal collaboration, it would be necessary to develop elaborate procedures and controls which would not only be less effective but probably so expensive as to offset any savings that had been anticipated; in other words, necessary integration of the system would have to be achieved mechanically through complicated administrative contrivance.

This kind of organization would deprive the supervisors and buyers of much of the responsibility they now have because it would deny them direct access to and control over some of the functions that are necessary for achieving satisfactory merchandising results. Friction and conflict would develop between the buying departments and the functional departments that would require the frequent intervention of the merchandising vice president or of some additional staff specialists he might find it necessary to employ to assist him in coordination. Thus, effective responsibility would move to a higher level in the organization and would probably come to rest ultimately with the merchandising vice president himself. The administrative unit would no longer be the individual buying department but the entire parent merchandising organization.

Because of this vastly greater degree of centralization, the merchandising vice president would probably have to shorten his span of control by interjecting a new level of supervision between himself and his supervisors—perhaps by dividing the buying departments into five or six groups, each heading up to a group merchandise manager. Initiative likewise would move to higher and higher levels. The organization would lose much of its present drive and spontaneity, much of its present resourcefulness and adaptiveness, and much of the stimulation it now provides for personal growth and development. The superiority of the present system is clear, not only in "human" terms but in terms of productive performance as well.

It should be noted that in the system as it now stands the necessary over-all "functional coordination" is adequately provided through the four functional assistants to the merchandising vice president. But these men and their offices are strictly "staff"; they are not in the line of authority and they in no way undermine the integrity of the relationship between the vice president and the supervisor, or between the supervisor and his own functional staff.

In a complex organization certain activities must be separated out and assigned to functional specialists. The question is, where are these functional specialists to be placed in the organization structure? Are they to be grouped together into specialized functional departments, or are they to be assigned directly to the central activity it is their purpose to serve? In the case of the parent merchandising organization of Sears, Roebuck and Co. that central activity is the buying and distribution of merchandise. The functions are therefore grouped around that central activity. This is the only relationship that makes sense: function to purpose. The relation of function to function is a meaningless abstraction—and needlessly complicated in practice.

V

People in management talk a great deal about the importance of delegation and are often critical of their subordinates for failing to exercise the responsibility supposedly delegated to them. But if an organization is set up along strictly functional lines, no amount of policy pronouncement, exhortation, or "supervisory training" can make it possible for supervisors to exercise anything approaching real responsibility. Failure to assume delegated responsibility is no doubt often a matter of individual temperament, but in many cases the structure of the organization itself makes significant delegation impossible, regardless of how much management may wish to delegate and regardless of how willing and even anxious subordinates may be to accept larger measures of responsibility.

Much of the vast scale of organization that is characteristic of modern industry, much of the tendency toward centralization of authority and responsibility, much of the growing impersonality and abstractness of working relationships are a result not so much of economic and technical factors as of the unhappy and often unnecessary principle of functional organization. The alternative is to group activities according to the purpose they serve rather than on the basis of their technical similarities. And a corollary is to seek that particular configuration of activity assignments that will permit effective authority and responsibility to be vested at the lowest possible levels in the organization. By the proper application of this principle, it should be possible to preserve the economic and technical advantages of large-scale enterprise, which are often very great, and at the same time restore many of the essential human values that can be realized only within relatively small working groups. Herein lies a fruitful field for creative management action.

People in the Structure

I

A favorite concept of scientific management, introduced well
after Taylor's time but in tune with his thinking, is the limited
"span of control." Under this concept, which has many weighty
supporters, "The number of subordinates whose tasks are
inter-dependent who can be directed immediately and effectively by one individual is strictly limited. . . . It should not
exceed five or six."[1] This theory was first expressed by the late
General Sir Ian Hamilton as a rule for military organization.
It was elaborated and first applied to problems of business
organization by a leader of the British school of scientific
management, Lyndall Urwick.

Urwick's confidence in the theory was greatly increased by
a friend, A. V. Graicunas, who demonstrated mathematically
that the number of cross relationships within and between a
group of subordinates and their superior varies geometrically
with the number of subordinates. Thus, with a supervisor and
four subordinates, the number of direct, cross, and group

[1] Lyndall Urwick, "Executive Decentralization with Functional Coordination," *The Management Review,* December 1935, p. 356.

relationships is 44. Adding one additional subordinate brings the number of relationships to 100. With six subordinates, the number jumps to about 200, and with seven to between 450 and 500.[2] So expressed, the consequence of lengthening an executive's span of control appear formidable indeed.

It is only common sense that there must be *some* limit *somewhere* to the number of people whose work one person can supervise and direct. Without doubt, many business executives today are laboring under spans of control that are entirely too wide. This is probably one of the causes of strain and overwork which is the executive's occupational hazard. It is also a frequent source of organizational inefficiency, because in trying to deal with too many subordinates the executive becomes a bottleneck. Subordinates are unable to clear with him things that need his approval, decisions are delayed and work held up, and the executive himself is prevented by sheer lack of time from giving attention to important matters to which only he can attend.

These things occur with sufficient frequency to lend plausibility to the idea of a limited span. But whether they justify a limitation as severe as "not more than five or six" is another question. As Urwick himself has written, it "is not a rigid rule to be applied woodenly in all situations. But it is a very useful general principle and a valuable diagnostic instrument in cases where organizational weakness exists."[3] Granted its usefulness in this sense, the proponents of the span of control theory have never really worked out the variety of factors which enter into determining the numbers of people who can be supervised effectively in different types of circumstances. Instead, the emphasis is constantly on *shortening* the span, without giving much more than lip service to the fact that

[2] Lyndall Urwick, "The Manager's Span of Control," *Harvard Business Review,* May–June 1956, p. 41.

[3] *Ibid.,* p. 41.

circumstances often differ and that under certain conditions there may be positive advantages in *lengthening* the span. Nor is recognition given to the fact that some of the elements requiring shorter spans are themselves subject to modification, with potential improvements of great significance to the organization and the people in it. An adequate span of control theory would take all of these factors into account and not merely those which argue for limitation.

II

One such factor is the desirability of holding down the number of administrative levels in the organization. If applied literally, the span of control theory would increase substantially the number of such levels in an organization of any size. "Layering" of this kind carries with it certain serious liabilities.

In terms of administrative levels, we may conceive of two different types of organization structure. One such structure, with a limited span of control and a large number of administrative levels, might be called "tall" or "vertical." The other, with a broad span of control and fewer levels, might be called "flat" or "horizontal."

In the vertical structure there is greater "administrative distance" between top and bottom, between the responsible head of the organization and the people performing the actual tasks which are the organization's reason for being. In sociology, there is a concept of "social distance," of which the concept of "administrative distance" may be considered a special case. One consequence of social distance is to magnify problems of communication. So too with administrative distance. In the vertical structure the administrator is forced to rely less on knowledge growing out of direct contact and more on formal reporting systems and information which is filtered up to him through successive levels of supervision and perhaps considerably distorted in the process. A great deal is lost if the facts about problems have to work their way up through too many hands—and too many "censors"—before they reach the man who has to act on them. Furthermore, less frequent contact with people in the lower levels of the organization necessarily renders the administrator's leadership more tenuous, more impersonal, and thereby less effective.

A good administrator will still find means of maintaining touch with as many people as possible and as far down in the organization as possible. But there is a marked difference in the nature of the relationship between the top man and those at lower levels if there are one or more formal layers between them. Much of the impersonality for which business is often criticized, much of the lack of mutual understanding between workers and management which is of concern to many thoughtful observers, traces to excessive administrative distance and consequent difficulties of communication. And be it emphasized that this administrative distance is as serious a barrier to the understanding of workers by management as it is to the understanding of management by workers. At each extremity, administrative as well as social distance distorts perceptions of, and inhibits identification with, those at the opposite pole.

A further difficulty of the vertical structure with a limited span of control is that it tends to remove the process of decision making from the scene of action and to concentrate it at higher levels. This, of course, is one aspect of the limitations such a structure places on the opportunities for effective decentralization. Especially in complex situations with many unpredictable elements requiring judgment, there are great advantages in relying primarily on the individuals closest to the scene of action and in not restricting too narrowly their range of discretion.

There are two criteria by which the decisions people make

are generally evaluated: first, was the decision objectively right, that is, right in terms of circumstances and results? And second, did it meet with the approval of someone higher up the line? The two criteria are not necessarily equivalent. One of the values of the flat organization and of maximum delegation of authority lies in the fact that a higher proportion of decisions is likely to be judged by the first criterion. One of the difficulties of the vertical structure is that more decisions have to meet *both* criteria. As a matter of fact, providing such checks and balances is one of the primary reasons for establishing the hierarchical types of structure. The difficulty is that such structures remove those reviewing the decisions of their subordinates farther from the scene of action and bring much more frequently into play the points of view of other persons whose thinking may be equally "right" but different.

Centralization, while sometimes efficient for the accomplishment of a specific task, is at a great disadvantage in dealing with the problem of change, which is a major characteristic of modern society, particularly in the economic field. The vertical type of structure seriously impairs the ability of the organization to adapt to new conditions. Not only is this a result of the tendency to concentrate decision making at higher levels; the functionalization which is characteristic of tall structures develops specialists rather than generalists, and specialists are likely to see problems from their own particular angles of vision which may not always be as objective as circumstances require. The complexity of the functionalized organization may make change slow, difficult, and incomplete.

It is harder to get new ideas adopted in the vertical organization because of its greater rigidity and more stubborn resistance to change. More clearances are necessary, more preconceived notions have to be overcome. There are more people at higher levels who may seek to appropriate new ideas for self-aggrandizement or bury them for self-protection, either of which is likely to smother the generation of new ideas at lower levels.

It is easier to correct mistakes in the flat type of structure. Not only is such a structure more flexible, but fewer people have their personal or positional prestige involved in policies or actions which events may prove to be wrong. Thus, more people in the organization can look at things objectively, and it is easier to "back water" if necessary.

Considerations such as these are of sufficient moment to warrant careful exploration of means by which the number of administrative levels, the administrative distance, can be held to the irreducible minimum. A clue for this purpose is imbedded in the span of control theory itself.

The theory explicitly recognizes that the degree of interdependence between the work of subordinates must be taken into account. Urwick's definitive wording of the concept reads: "No superior can supervise directly the work of more than five or, at the most, six subordinates *whose work interlocks*."[4] This is an important qualification, too important to serve merely as a convenient explanation for the fact that the rule of "not more than five or six" is so frequently violated in actual business practice. The real significance of the qualification is its implicit suggestion that broader spans of control, and hence shorter administrative distances, are possible if the work of subordinates can be made *less* interlocking, *less* interdependent. This in turn suggests the need for greater administrative decentralization, for so organizing the business that individual units and divisions can function with maximum self-sufficiency and with the least possible need for specific administrative coordination and control. Some of the possibilities along this line have already been indicated.

In the case of the Sears parent buying organization, for example, it is quite true that the present very broad span of

[4] *Ibid.* (Urwick's italics).

control is possible primarily because only modest amounts of coordination are required between departments. The hardware department, for example, can go its own way without too much regard for what is happening in the yard goods department. Closer coordination is required between the work of departments handling related lines of merchandise, as in the case of home furnishings or major appliances, but even so each individual department, by the very nature of the merchandising business, can function with a considerable degree of independence. The situation may be otherwise in, for example, a factory organization, for there many departments are likely to work in "series," whereas merchandising departments work in "parallel." If a department at one stage of the manufacturing process gets off schedule or does careless work, other departments will suffer. To guard against such contingencies, closer supervision and control are necessary, which means shorter spans of control and more layers of supervision.

But it need not necessarily follow from this that the span of control of the Sears merchandising organization would *have* to be as broad as it is. On the contrary, the only reason such a span is possible at all is the fact that the work of the individual departments is highly decentralized. As the analysis in the preceding chapter has shown, this decentralization depends in turn on a substantial modification of the classical principle of functional organization.

So, too, with factory organizations. No doubt, there is a constitutional necessity for shorter spans than are possible in merchandising. The determining factor in the structure of any organization is the technology it employs, and the technologies of factories will vary greatly according to processes and equipment, types of skill, market characteristics, and so forth. The nature of the technology will make a relatively broad span of control possible in one instance and necessitate a much shorter span in another.

Even so, for any particular technology, there is a range of possibilities. Given the identical technical conditions, one organization can be set up on a broad, flat basis and another on a tall, vertical basis. The difference will depend on the degree to which all possible means of administrative decentralization are employed, which turns largely on the extent to which all necessary specialized activities are directly related to central productive functions and made subordinate to such functions. To the extent that specialized activities are separated from central functions and grouped into specialized departments, the possibilities of effective decentralization are diminished, with consequent necessity for limiting spans of control and lengthening chains of command.

III

The essential error of the generally accepted span of control theory is its implicit assumption that the superior must not only direct the work of his subordinates but must mediate many of the relationships between them. The mathematical calculation of the geometric progression in the number of relationships as subordinates are added suggests a skeptical attitude toward the ability of subordinates to cooperate spontaneously without the intervention of the superior.

A narrow span of control is not only appropriate but essential if subordinates are expected to do nothing except at the specific direction of a superior and within a narrow framework of policy and procedures closely controlled by higher authority. There are organizations where conditions of this kind obtain: for example, government service. By the very nature of our Constitutional system, authority flows from the top down. Every action taken by a government agency or a government employee must be clearly related to the chain of authority that legitimatizes that action. Furthermore, the amount of initiative and independent judgment permitted public officials is severely restricted, as of course it should be.

Thus, in government organizations we cannot expect to have the breadth of control that is possible in private organizations. By the same token, we must reconcile ourselves to considerable elaboration in the supervisory hierarchies of government bureaus. Only by this means can we assure the observance of proper Constitutional and legal procedures and preserve the concept of a government of laws and not of men. Nevertheless, governmental spans of control are considerably shorter and governmental hierarchies considerably more elaborate than they *need* to be. This is partly in consequence of the influence of the span of control theory, but it is chiefly due to the extent to which the concept of functional organization has been applied to government organization. When all this is said, however, the fact remains that a substantial degree of structural complexity is a functional necessity in government operations.

This only serves to highlight the greater appropriateness and desirability of relatively broad spans of control and relatively simple organizational structures where there is an advantage in giving subordinates room for the exercise of independent judgment and initiative. The justification for broader spans of control rests on the assumption that at least as far as private industry is concerned the primary motive force of the organization is the initiative and drive and intelligence of the people in the organization; that these do not have to be imposed from the top down; and that the chief function of the leader is to channel and direct and imaginatively utilize that motive force.

Perhaps the classic example of the flat type of organization structure is to be found at Sears, Roebuck and Co. Note has already been taken of the parent merchandising organization, where forty-four senior executives report directly to a single officer. In a typical retail store there are forty-odd department managers reporting to a single store manager or, in some cases, to a single merchandise manager. This type of structure violates the basic tenet of the span of control theory because more people are assigned to key executives than they can easily supervise and control. But there are positive advantages in such a system precisely because it tends to *avoid* too close supervision and control.

The amount of time these superior executives can devote to any of their subordinates is, on the average, limited. Under these circumstances, the only possible way for them to accomplish the jobs for which they are responsible is to have people in the subordinate positions who can take responsibility, who can be trusted to use good judgment, and who can move ahead on their own without having to clear everything in advance. The only way for the store manager to do a successful hardware business is find or develop a highly skilled hardware merchant for that department. The only way for the merchandising vice president to build volume and profit in the refrigerator business is to find or develop a skilled appliance merchandiser who knows how to build volume and profit without having to have very much of the thinking done for him.

If one or more levels of supervision were interjected between these top men and their subordinates, there would still be a premium on having good department heads but not as great a premium as there is now. Instead, there would be more pressure for outstanding people at the intermediary levels. These people would be responsible for the performance of *groups* of departments, and it is to them, not the managers or supervisors of the individual departments, that the superiors would look primarily for results. This shift in the primary concern of the top man would have a tendency toward deterioration of quality at the department level—not because the top man was consciously content with lower quality people there but simply because he was relieved to some extent from the compelling necessity for high quality.

But other influences are also at work. In the present extremely flat structures, good people in subordinate positions are exposed to a quality of experience that tends to develop their capacities in a singularly effective manner. They are *forced* to assume responsibility. They cannot be running constantly to superiors for approval of their actions; they have to make their own decisions and stand or fall by the results. In the process, they make mistakes—but that, too, contributes to their growth and maturity.

The limited span of control makes it difficult for subordinate executives to get too far off base or to stay off base too long. But precisely for this reason, subordinates in such a system are deprived of one of their most valuable means of learning. For people learn as much—perhaps more—from their mistakes as from their successes. This is one of the root problems of modern organization: that people have been so hemmed in by supervision and controls that they have too little opportunity to move ahead on their own. If the opportunity for initiative and independent judgment is real and not fictitious, it always carries with it the danger, even the probability, that people will make mistakes. But if they are too closely guarded against that danger, they may be denied the means of growth and development.

It is just barely conceivable that a child could be so protected that it would never be in danger of being run over by a car, or falling out of a tree and breaking its leg, or drowning in the lake, or meeting any of the other disasters, fatal or otherwise, to which childhood is subject. Perhaps the child *could* be protected to this extent, but if so it would never grow up into an adult, responsible human being; it would never be more than a weak and worrisome thing. If children are to grow up into competent, self-respecting, self-reliant adults, they have to have room to grow, which means room to fail as well as succeed.

A loosely structured, highly permissive system of organization is not an easy one to live in—any more than growing up is easy. Not everyone can function effectively in such a system. It requires a large measure of self-reliance, self-confidence, and personal capacity; those who do not possess such qualities in adequate degree tend to be weeded out—in fact, *have* to be weeded out if the system is to work. But in this kind of organization people are encouraged, even pushed, to reach to the limit of their capacities, and sometimes to develop capacities they never knew they had. Herein lies perhaps the greatest advantage of loosely knit organization structures with broad spans of control: the superior opportunities they provide for personal growth.

Modern management is deeply concerned with the need for providing assured and orderly sources of qualified executive manpower as one of the vital conditions for economic survival. Extensive and elaborate programs are often devised for this purpose. The relationship between organization structure and executive development, however, is often overlooked.

Some degree of organized effort and systematic procedure is necessary, but these are not the essence of an executive development program. That program must be built around the dynamic forces which foster the processes of growth and maturation. Growth occurs *within* the individual. It can be encouraged or inhibited by external conditions, but the organism itself must do the growing. Properly conceived, an executive training program must be directed toward stimulating and releasing the growth potentialities of individuals. Far more is involved than mere imparting of knowledge. What is needed is the opportunity for "creative experience," to borrow Mary Parker Follett's telling phrase.

The opportunity for this kind of experience depends in con-siderable part on the structure of the organization within which the individual functions. The future executive needs practice in making decisions. He needs to become accustomed to carrying responsibility. He needs the experience of making mistakes and having to live with them. He needs the courage that comes from facing new problems and solving them. People of promise are more likely to be exposed to conditions of this kind at a much earlier age in organizations character-ized by broad spans of control and extensive managerial de-centralization. If they have to wait until middle age before having a chance to carry bona fide responsibility, they are not likely to develop into strong, self-reliant leaders and execu-tives.

IV

A decentralized system does not involve blind delegation. The superior must have confidence in his subordinates, but he cannot afford to misplace that confidence. Even if he dele-gates, he is still responsible. The most important kind of de-cision he has to make as administrator is in whom he will place his confidence and how far. He must have a sure instinct as to which individuals can move ahead on their own and which require help. A considerable part of his time must be devoted to working with newer subordinates or those who otherwise need special support. But throughout, the emphasis must be placed on developing individual competence, bringing people along to the point where they can handle the responsibilities of their jobs with a minimum of direction and supervision.

If for any reason a superior loses confidence in a subordi-nate, the subordinate loses his usefulness and his ability to function. Effective leadership in this kind of organization is not easy. In structures with many checks and balances and an extensive system of controls, people can be supported to a considerable extent by the structure itself. But in an organization that places a premium on people who can stand on their own feet, the top man in the unit must be pretty hard-boiled if he becomes convinced they cannot.

The factor of confidence is crucial, because without it effective delegation is impossible. An incident in the life of Abraham Lincoln affords a classic example. In the early years of the Civil War, and particularly in his dealings with McClellan and Halleck, Lincoln was forced to intervene frequently and in detail in matters of military strategy and tactics. After the emergence of Grant, in whom he soon had full confidence, he left the military conduct of the war almost wholly in his hands. In April 1864 Lincoln wrote Grant:

Not expecting to see you again before the Spring Campaign begins, I wish to express in this way my entire satisfaction with what you have done up to this time so far as I understand it. The particulars of your plan I neither know nor seek to know. You are vigilant and self-reliant, and, pleased with this, I wish not to obtrude any constraints or restraints upon you. While I am very anxious that any great disaster or capture of our men in great numbers shall be avoided, I know these points are less likely to escape your attention than they would mine. If there is anything wanting which is within my power to give, do not fail to let me know it. And now, with a brave Army and a just cause, may God sustain you.[5]

Another aspect of the significance of confidence in delegation is illustrated by the organization of the civilian branches of the federal government. If a superior is to have complete confidence in his subordinates, he must have some measure of control over who his subordinates are. He must have a degree of freedom in their selection, their discipline, and if necessary their transfer or dismissal. The federal civil service system, however, places restrictions on such freedom. These restric-

[5] Quoted in Lord Charwood, *Abraham Lincoln* (New York: Pocket Books, Inc., 1939), p. 433.

tions undeniably serve a useful purpose, by providing a necessary minimum of security for government personnel and an essential safeguard for the career service. They have the unfortunate consequence, however, of creating a condition which greatly inhibits the delegation of authority and responsibility. Even where other factors might permit delegation, its practice is limited because the superior has so little control over his subordinates. These people may be highly skilled; they may be the soul of integrity and of dedication to public service. But the superior knows if one of them does not measure up there is not much he can do about it. And he knows, too, that however much confidence he may have in his *present* subordinate staff, his freedom of choice will be limited if replacements are necessary and he may find himself with someone in whom, for whatever reason, justified or not, he cannot feel fully confident. Under such circumstances, he is likely to be reluctant to delegate what might otherwise be in his power to delegate.

On the side of the subordinates themselves in government there are elements which inhibit their acceptance of responsibility. By and large there is considerably more turnover among higher government officials than there is at comparable levels in private business. This poses a serious problem for people in subordinate positions, for they can never be sure that the next man to sit in the superior's seat will approve of actions they take with the approval of their present superiors.

Observers of government operations are frequently struck by the amount of red tape involved, the number of approvals and countersignatures necessary for even the simplest actions, the number of people who are consulted, and the complicated business of "going through channels." To a considerable extent, this kind of behavior is self-protective. This is not to imply that government workers are any less self-reliant than their counterparts in private industry, or that they have any innate proclivities for paper work or procedural formality. Rather, it is simply a form of adaptive behavior in response to an objective condition of government employment. The acceptance of too much personal responsibility is likely to be dangerous, and those who do not exercise due caution in that respect are not likely to last very long. Hence the need to diffuse responsibility, to secure multiple clearances and approvals, to make sure everything goes through the right channels and that every action is properly "documented." In other words, confidence is important for the subordinate as well as the superior. Under the conditions of government service, confidence on the part of both parties is more difficult to establish than in private industry—not because of any human weakness but because of the nature of the system.

V

Effective leadership in a loosely knit organization with a broad span of control requires men with a certain kind of temperament and a certain kind of attitude toward people. Managers who are most successful are likely to take a great deal of pride in their unit and their employees. But this pride is not indiscriminate. Such managers hold their people to high standards and are critical of those who fail to measure up. They are usually good judges of people, able to evaluate their strengths and weaknesses, and to deal with them accordingly. In part because of their skill on this score, such managers usually *do* have people in whom they can take pride. Because they are good judges of men, they can delegate responsibilities with confidence.

The manager who is less skilled at judging men or who has basic attitudes of distrust toward other people is not likely to operate effectively in this kind of system because he cannot delegate with confidence. If he finds himself in such an organization (and stays in it) one or both of two things will probably happen. The man will overwork himself trying to maintain the broad span, or he will add staff to help him carry the load. Because he has little confidence in people, because he feels that people have to be closely supervised, he will move toward a system in which he and a few key people at the top can do the "real thinking" and set up necessary controls to make sure that those further down the line carry out their instructions. This kind of manager, in other words, simply sets up the kind of organization in which he can function most effectively and most comfortably—assuming he has the necessary latitude to arrange things to fit his temperament; if he is unduly restricted in this, he may run into trouble, ulcers or otherwise.

Managers who are able to work effectively and comfortably in the broad, flat type of organization relinquish none of their responsibility for guidance and direction or for final results, but they seek to capitalize on the initiative and good sense of their subordinates rather than trying to do all the "real thinking" for them. Their primary method of solving problems is working with the people involved, to the end of solving not only the immediate problem but of strengthening the ability of their subordinates to deal with other problems in the future. To this end, they like to work directly with the heads of subordinate units rather than through an intermediate staff. If the organization is not already fairly broad, with extensive delegation, they are likely to try to move in that direction if they are permitted any latitude in organizational arrangements. They can probably function in a more centralized and more hierarchical structure, and function quite well because of the kind of persons they are, but probably not with the personal stimulation and satisfaction the other kind of system provides.

Thus the problem of organization structure is not merely a technical matter of how functions and activities are arranged and related to each other. The task of changing an established structure is considerably more involved than issuing a directive and redrawing the organization chart. The way any organization is set up is likely to reflect the personality and temperament of the key people in it—above all, the personality and temperament of the man at the top.

The broad, flat type of organization structure is most likely to be developed by managements characterized by a basic orientation of confidence in the good sense and good judgment of people, in their integrity, and in their ability to handle large measures of responsibility with a minimum of supervision and control. Once in being, the very nature of such an organization structure tends to *force* top executives to concern themselves primarily with people. Store problems or merchandising problems or manufacturing problems have to be looked upon as problems of people rather than problems of things. If the performance of a department is unsatisfactory, the only way to correct it is to straighten out the management of the department. It is not enough to correct the immediate problem; the important thing is to work toward strengthening the management of subordinate units so that such units can handle their own problems without constant recourse to intervention or support from higher management.

An essential characteristic of the system is the manner in which it challenges people, gives them a chance to grow. This characteristic is not achieved without cost, and that cost is that not everybody can make good. The surprising thing is the extent to which even average people are encouraged, sometimes pushed, to reach to the limit of their capacities. For every one who cannot make good there are many more who achieve levels of personal growth they could not have reached if the system were weighted down with crutches and safe-guards.

America has prospered and grown great, spiritually as well as materially, because we have a kind of political and economic system that has high expectations of people, that stretches people to their utmost. The type of organization structure and executive leadership here discussed compares closely with basic characteristics of American society and with main currents in American historical development.

A. B. Guthrie, Jr., in his novel, *The Way West,* tells of a plodding Missourian, debating whether or not to join a wagon train scheduled to leave for Oregon in the spring of 1845: "What he needed was a dare. What he needed was to find out what he amounted to." This is what most of us need—a dare, a challenge, a test to see what we amount to. This is much more likely to be provided by an organization which is constructed on the basis of a deep and abiding faith in the capacities of men and women than by one which is skeptical of such capacities and seeks to compensate for human weakness rather than capitalize on human strength.

Chapter EIGHT

The Symbols Men Work By

Every action of management has two aspects, one "technical," the other "symbolic." The technical aspect is the objective nature of the action. The symbolic aspect is the meaning imputed to the action. Every action of management is evaluated by workers in both its technical and symbolic aspects: what *is* it? and what does it *mean?*

I

A worker's earnings, for example, are not only his source of livelihood; they are also an important factor in his psychic well-being, for their amount tells him a great deal about what the management of the company (and to a large extent his fellow workers) think of him and his value to the organization. It makes a great difference whether pay scales in a plant are pitched high or low by community standards, or whether the rates for a particular job are relatively high or low in comparison with other jobs in the plant.

· This is why job evaluation plans so often create intense emotional disturbances. Jobs are not merely sets of duties and responsibilities whose components can be described and measured; they also define the status of workers in the organization. Any effort to "analyze" jobs for the purpose of placing them in proper rank, one with the other, carries the clear implication that the present ranking, in someone's mind, needs changing. Workers find little comfort in the assurance that no incumbent's rate will be reduced, even though a lower ranking may be assigned to the job as a result of the analysis. The fact remains that a worker's job may be relegated to a lower plane, and you cannot depreciate what he *does* without depreciating *him* in the process.

The installation of a job evaluation program is itself a matter of prime symbolic significance. Does management feel that the workers are being overpaid and is this an effort to get more work out of them for the same or less money? Or is it an effort to straighten out a set of rates that the workers themselves recognize as jumbled and to replace them with a wage structure that is fair and just? The difference in worker reactions will be great, depending on whether they view management's motives in the former or in the latter light.

Their view will depend primarily on their previous experience with management. If management's past actions have given them grounds for confidence, they are likely to accept the plan with confidence and as a further expression of management's concern for fairness. If management's past actions have given them grounds for distrust, they will probably react with suspicion and antagonism. In any action affecting workers it is good procedure and sound common sense to explain what is being done and why; but no amount of explanation is likely to be of much reassurance if the past experience of workers has given them cause to be wary of management's intentions.

The techniques employed for evaluating jobs are of little significance to the workers, except insofar as they tend to confirm or deny conjectures as to management's motives. One of the great difficulties of some of the more popular systems of job evaluation is that the methods used are so complex that the workers do not understand them. The resulting distrust is likely to strengthen any suspicions of management they may already have. If workers are asked to accept something on faith, they must have grounds for faith.

Precisely because of the profound symbolic significance of wage rates, it is important to workers (even more than to management) that the rates be orderly, that they "make sense," that they be "fair." The chief virtue of a job evaluation plan lies in the fact that it is (or at least should be) tangible evidence of management's concern that its wage structure meet these criteria.

Individual merit increases and the company's system for granting them are also of symbolic importance. The fact that one worker may get increases more frequently or in greater amounts than others speaks volumes, not merely as to how management appraises the economic value of the members of a work group but as to how it appraises them as persons. Earnings differentials have the effect of ranking the members of the work group in relation to each other. Generally speaking, this ranking reflects *management's* perspective. The workers, however, look on the various jobs and the various members of the group from a somewhat different perspective. Where this difference results in two systems of ranking, friction and dissatisfaction are the likely result.

The symbolic function of wages can be illustrated by an experience common to all organizations that use merit increases as the primary means for adjusting employee earnings but from time to time grant general increases to adjust rates to changes, say, in living costs or competitive conditions. In such cases, the general increase has relatively little significance to the individual worker. It may have an over-all significance in that it tells the workers as a group something of how alert management is to changes that affect them, but it does not have the *personal* impact of the individual increase. Most executives in companies using the merit system could probably relate instances of employees who, upon requesting a raise and being reminded of having recently benefited from a general increase, reply, "Oh, but *everyone* got that."

A few years ago a prominent labor leader, in the course of a discussion with a group of businessmen, pointed out the symbolic function of wages as illustrated by what he termed the "unsophisticated attitude" of workers toward wage increases. They are likely to be quite happy, he noted, over a 5 per cent increase despite the fact that prices may also have gone up 5 per cent. But they will be insulted by an offer of one per cent if prices are stable and will be violently opposed to a 2 per cent decrease even if prices have dropped by 10 per cent. The symbolism of wages is a "fact of life" in industrial relations which labor leaders as well as businessmen must take into account.

Concern for the symbolic aspects of compensation is not restricted to rank-and-file workers; in fact, it is likely to be most intense among executives. As one moves from the lower to the higher levels of the management hierarchy, status differentials become increasingly important. In part, this is because fewer people perform similar functions and there is greater need for *individual* as compared with *group* distinctions. The system of status symbols is therefore usually more complex at the higher levels. This applies not only to such matters as titles and office appointments; it applies above all to salaries. Salaries are the indisputable measure of relative standing within an organization. As Peter Drucker has pointed out, the principal reason for the very high amounts often paid to the chief executives of large organizations lies in the fact that only by having a wide range between the lowest and the highest management jobs is it possible to reflect all the distinctions in rank between members of the management group. This symbolic function of executive salaries is not impaired by high income taxes. Even if the greater part of an executive's salary is taxed away, it has already served its purpose of defining where he stands in the organization.

Another reason for the greater concern of management people with matters of salary lies in the fact that so many of them are mobile, and frequency and amount of salary increases are the most tangible and perhaps the most reliable indication of the individual's "progress." Failure to receive an increase for an undue period of time, or receiving a smaller increase than expected, are thus matters of serious concern and strong reaction.

In a broad sense, from the standpoint of the recipients, the primary function of wages and salaries is symbolic rather than economic. Beyond their status-defining functions within the organization, they are the means by which people acquire the symbols which define the kinds of people they are and the places they occupy in society. The component of wages or salaries which is truly economic, in the sense of providing the means for maintaining life, is relatively small; it is the *way of life* that is expensive. This way of life is expressed largely through such symbols as kind of house and neighborhood lived in, grades of clothing worn, modes of recreation and so forth, all of them usually well above the levels physiologically necessary for the preservation of life and health. Symbols which help define status within organizations and in the community cannot be dismissed as externals. They are external only in the sense that they are the outer, visible expression of the kinds of persons people conceive of themselves as being, playing the kinds of roles they see as right and proper for them. The status symbols they acquire are the external evidence, to others and to *themselves,* of the kind of people they *really* are.

Wages and salaries and the things derived from them are certainly not the only symbols of status, but in a business enterprise they are probably the most important—much more important than in other kinds of enterprises, such as education, government, or the military services which are not based so strictly on a monetary rationale. Therefore, a management which considers only the technical aspect of its compensation system may unknowingly invite serious repercussions—and be amazed at the intensity and "irrationality" of the worker's reactions.

Economic science has always been unsure of itself when it has tried to move from the simple concepts of economic motivations to the complexities of actual behavior. The reason for this unsureness lies in the fact that economic motivations are *always secondary,* always subservient to considerations of ego sustenance. "Noneconomic behavior" can make sense from this point of view, but from that of the classical economist it must forever remain an aberration. Just as material prosperity can never be sufficient because wants are insatiable, so wage and salary rates can never be adequate in a *technical* sense, but they can be and often are adequate in a *symbolic* sense. Marxian and related theories of the class struggle, as well as more modern and more orthodox theories of economic behavior, fail to appreciate this distinction, and because they do so they fail to account for the course of social history and are a misleading guide for social action.

II

Employee benefit plans have traditionally been looked upon by management as a means for improving employee relations. Long before so-called "fringe benefits" became a common subject for collective bargaining, group insurance, group hospitalization, profit sharing, pensions, illness and separation allowances, paid holidays and vacations, and similar measures had become standard features of modern personnel practice. Despite the increasing frequency of union demands in this area, the greater part of expenditure for such purposes is at management's initiative and represents, in the logic of management, an investment in employee good will.

The usual theory on which management operates is that employees will appreciate management's generosity and that their gratitude will conduce to improved morale and higher productivity. Unfortunately, this simple cause-and-effect relationship seldom works out in practice, and if management, in the way it introduces the benefit or talks about it, creates the impression that it expects appreciation, the reaction of employees is likely to be exactly the opposite.

Typically, new benefit plans installed in organizations already enjoying good employee relations are greeted with favor. Typically, also, new plans installed in organizations where employee relations are poor are greeted with resentment. Substantially the identical benefit plan can serve to improve morale in one situation and weaken it in another, depending on the quality of employee relations existing at the time the plans are introduced.

The indirect and conditional nature of the influence of benefit plans on employee attitudes may be illustrated by reference to the Sears Profit Sharing Plan. The plan was installed in 1916, long before projects of this type had gained much currency in business practice. Over the years, the plan has grown to substantial proportions. At the end of 1958, it had assets of over $1 billion. Through the plan the employees own about one fourth of all outstanding company stock and thus, as a group, are the largest stockholders of the company.

The significance of the plan to employees is best exemplified, not by over-all figures such as these, but by actual examples of typical employee experiences. One young woman left to be married after nine years in the fund. During these nine years she herself had deposited $1,120 in profit sharing, but she withdrew on leaving $4,025. A woman who had been a member of the fund for twenty-five years deposited $3,450 and withdrew $47,125. A man who had made a lifetime career with Sears and who had been a member of profit sharing since its inception deposited $4,820. When he retired his share of the fund was valued at $174,980. These cases are typical. It has not been unusual for employees who have retired in recent years and who have been in the fund since the beginning to withdraw on leaving more than they have earned in wages during their entire working lives.

Unquestionably, the profit sharing plan has had a highly favorable influence on the attitudes of Sears employees. It is the most talked about of all company policies. Employees are not around long before they begin to hear about the plan from their fellow workers. The nature of the plan is explained to new employees as part of the regular induction procedure, and its current operations are reviewed once a year with all members at the time they receive their personal annual statements. But the plan does not need to be "sold"; the employees take care of that themselves—much more effectively than would be possible for management.

Nevertheless, it is clear that there is not a direct one-two relationship between the plan and the high employee morale with which it is associated. For one thing, few employees have any notion, except within fairly wide limits, of the extent of their own personal holdings. This fact seems to indicate they have considerable confidence in the way the fund is being managed. But it also indicates that the significance of the plan to employees lies not so much in the value of their individual holdings as in the fact that the very existence of the fund is tangible evidence that the company is run with consideration for their welfare, that the interest of management in making profits is in their own interest as well. The values of the plan are thus primarily symbolic rather than economic.

This is not to minimize the importance of the economic values; the plan is effective symbolically in large part because it is so substantial economically. The existence of the plan and the substantial nature of its benefits tells employees a great deal about the kind of company they are working for and about the attitude of the company's management toward them as people.

The existence of the plan likewise says something of importance to management itself. Profit sharing has become so thoroughly embedded in the Sears tradition that management takes great pride in it and feels a heavy weight of responsibility for conducting the affairs of the company in such a way as to conserve and promote the interests of employees, both as employees per se and as members of the fund. It is a constant reminder to management that there is a wide overlap between the interests of stockholders and the interests of employees. In other words, the plan serves a symbolic function for management as well as for employees. Furthermore, management's pride in the plan encourages interest in all phases of management-employee relationships. Thus the attitude of pride is generalized, with important consequences for the atmosphere in which the work of the company is carried on.

It has become common in recent years for those steeped in the findings of human relations research to minimize the importance of economic factors such as wages and employee benefits to employee morale. A truer estimate would seem to be that these factors are of great importance, but in a manner quite different from that customarily conceived. If these factors are looked at from the standpoint of their symbolic rather than their economic functions, their significance emerges in a clearer light.

III

Some managements have spent considerable sums of money installing clean, modern washrooms on the assumption that this will help improve employee morale. That there is some relationship is undeniable, but here again it is far from simple and direct. Undoubtedly poorly equipped and improperly maintained washrooms create resentment, but the thing chiefly resented is the attitude of management which holds employees in such disdain that it fails to provide them with the ordinary decencies. This attitude will probably express itself in other ways as well. Installing a new washroom may remove one specific cause for complaint, but unless there is a comparable change in other aspects of management behavior there will be no improvement in morale; employees will merely concentrate their resentment on other evidences of the poor regard in which management holds them.

Training has frequently been cited as a means for improving employee morale. With respect to induction training, the theory is that giving newcomers a better picture of the company—its organization, products, policies, and so forth—will create good will and enable employees to make a quicker adjustment to the job. With respect to job training, the theory is that the well-trained employee is not only more competent and more productive but also more satisfied. There is undoubtedly considerable justification for both these theories, but so far as morale is concerned there is a further factor of even greater importance. The fact that a company goes to some effort and expense to see that new employees are properly brought into the fold and carefully instructed in their work tells them that the company considers both them and their work of real importance. Where management makes no provision for matters such as these or handles them in a slipshod, haphazard fashion, the message to employees is likewise clear and unmistakable—and the reaction predictable.

The way jobs themselves are set up tells employees a great deal about management's attitudes. A popular current management practice is to emphasize, through house organs and otherwise, the importance of every job in the company. But unless jobs have real content, unless workers are expected to exercise judgment and initiative and to assume responsibility, the words management uses carry little conviction. Respect for employees is not merely a manner of personal behavior in their presence. Much more significant is the degree of respect implicit in the way work is organized. Jobs are given importance not by saying they are important but by making them important.

American management has displayed its characteristic inventive skill in the many devices that have been created to aid in the improvement of employee relations. The Sears profit sharing plan is only one such device. The McCormick Company's system of "multiple management" is another. The Western Electric interviewing program represents still another approach to the same end. Numerous other examples could be cited. Devices such as these are not only techniques; they are also symbols, rituals, ceremonials. But the important thing is neither the technique nor the ritual, but the spirit behind it.

The famous "Hawthorne Experiments" of the Western Electric Company a quarter of a century ago illustrate the fundamental importance of attitudes in contrast to actions. In an effort to determine the factors most conducive to higher employee productivity, a number of different steps were taken experimentally, and the results of each closely observed and recorded. Unfortunately for the original purpose of the research, *every* experimental step led to increased productivity, even when the step meant a marked change for the worse in working conditions. It became clear that the workers were responding not so much to what was actually done as to the fact that the experiments were being conducted at all; for they were tangible evidence of management's interest in and concern for its employees. The experiments provided little guidance as to what management should *do* but gave clear insight into what management should *be*.

Not only the words but the behavior of supervisors and executives express their attitudes toward their employees. Two executives in the same organization each made a practice of lunching periodically with a member of his staff. One executive always insisted on paying the check; the other always allowed his subordinate to pay. In each case, the action was intended, and accepted, as complimentary to the subordinate. Yet similar actions by other executives might well be interpreted as efforts to "bribe" or to "chisel."

In an employee attitude survey of a central warehouse, a considerable amount of resentment was expressed over the fact that the manager seldom spoke to employees except for straight business purposes. It was suggested to him that he be less aloof and at least make it a point to say "good morning." On a follow-up survey several weeks later employee resentment was at a boiling point—because the manager was saying "good morning" to each of them several times during the first hour or so of the day. The employees understood quite clearly from this that the manager was going through a perfunctory exercise; the fact that he said "good morning" more than once to the same person really meant that he failed to "see" the person. They already knew that they counted for little in his eyes. But it was adding insult to injury when he went through a form which, by its manner, emphasized still further his lack of awareness of them. The manager was hur-

riedly cautioned that unless he could remember whom he had
spoken to he had better stop saying "good morning" altogether.

IV

People cannot live or work together without each knowing
pretty well the attitude of the other. This applies in the home
and it applies in the work place. A husband and wife cannot
disguise for long their feelings for each other, nor parents and
children, nor managers and employees. One husband brings
his wife a beautiful bouquet of flowers, which she accepts as a
further expression of the love and devotion he holds for her.
Another husband brings his wife an equally beautiful bouquet
which causes her to wonder what he's been up to now. It is not
the beauty or the cost of the bouquet that is important, but
what it means—and the wife generally has a pretty good idea
on that score, as does the husband in interpreting his wife's
behavior toward him.

The reason *intent* is so important in all human relations is
that it is not actions themselves which are significant but their
meaning, and meaning is largely a function of intent. That
which gives a thing significance goes beyond the thing itself; it
is a "sign of" something and it is the "something" which is
important.

In their essence, industrial relations are not very different
from family relations. Some fathers try to "buy" the love and
affection of their wives and children, forgetting that love is a
reciprocal process and that respect and affection can only be
won to the extent they are given in return. Some managements,
like some fathers, try to find a cheap and easy substitute for
respect and are annoyed at the cheap and unsatisfactory response they obtain. Through generous wage scales, liberal
employee benefits, and attractive working conditions they
seek to buy the loyalty and good will of their employees and

thus avoid facing up to shortcomings of their own which may be at the root of employee unrest. Psychologically and morally, management's motives in installing an employee benefit plan or granting a general wage increase are sometimes the equivalent to those of a rich man who gives the preacher a sizable check and feels that he's done his duty to his church and his God for another year.

Managements sometimes indulge in various forms of "escapism." Such devices of modern personnel practice as morale surveys, psychological testing, merit rating, and the like can be used to help solve problems or to avoid them. A management that is troubled by the state of its employee relations may conduct a morale survey to secure facts on which it can act, or use the survey as an excuse for delaying action. Psychological tests may be a useful adjunct to selection processes or a substitute for responsible executive judgment. Merit rating may be a means for developing a rational compensation structure or a façade to disguise the need for more orderly compensation arrangements.

Under certain circumstances, even the establishment of a personnel department can be a form of "managerial escapism." This came out clearly in a study made a few years ago of two groups of relatively small retail stores. One group of stores had personnel managers; in the other group, personnel functions were performed by the managers themselves, with such clerical assistance as was necessary. There were marked differences in the levels of employee morale in the two groups of stores, but interestingly enough the differences were all in favor of the stores *without* personnel managers.

This did not mean that the presence of personnel managers was responsible for the lower morale; the chain of causation was quite otherwise. These were relatively small stores, small enough so that the managers should have been able to handle the personnel job themselves along with their merchandising and operating responsibilities. The fact that some managers felt it necessary to set up personnel departments really meant that they did not want to be bothered with what they considered the messy problems of dealing with people. This attitude of the managers—which inevitably reflected itself in many other ways—was responsible for the lower morale. The managers, in other words, were indulging in a form of "escapism" in an effort to avoid facing up to their own shortcomings and making the necessary changes in their own attitudes and ways of life.

The introduction of a new device or program (e.g., supervisory training) is sometimes almost fetishlike, not far removed psychologically from the offering of incantations or the burning of incense to ward off angry spirits. One difference between fetishism and Christianity is that Christianity postulates the unique responsibility of the individual soul; the prayer wheel is not enough. Management cannot afford prayer wheels; it must accept the unique, personal responsibility of individual managers for the character of their organizations and for the kind of experience their organizations provide for the people in them.

In this, managers may well be guided by the teachings of Jesus. One of the flaws of Pharisaism that Jesus attacked was its externalizing of religion. Pharisaism was so concerned with the forms of religious practice that it neglected the essence of religious life: the attitude of the spirit. But to Jesus the attitude of the spirit was all-important, and if a man's heart was right the external details would take care of themselves. What is true of religion is also true of management. If management's heart is not right, no excellence or skill in practice will make much difference. A moral fault cannot be remedied by technical contrivance. There is no substitute for character, no short cut to integrity.

There is no easy way to improve employee relations. Basically, the problem is moral and ethical. Attempts to deal with it without facing up to this fact are sterile. The material advances represented by higher wage scales, shorter hours, generous employee benefits, and better working conditions are all important, but none of them goes to the heart of the problem. And the heart of the problem is the hearts and souls of the individual men and women who comprise American industry.

Part THREE

*Business Citizenship and
American Democracy*

Chapter NINE

The Businessman as Citizen

I

The roles of citizen and businessman are not conflicting but complementary and mutually supporting—and in their essentials, inseparable.

There are important problem areas in contemporary society toward whose solution businessmen have an opportunity and an obligation to contribute significantly. They have an opportunity because these particular problems have an important bearing on the environment within which business enterprise functions. They have an obligation not only because they are citizens but because as businessmen they have certain resources and special competencies which need to be brought to bear if these problems are to be dealt with successfully.

Most of the problems of contemporary society arise from the successful solution of past problems. We would not, for example, be faced with a financial crisis in higher education if we were not well along the road toward providing virtually universal access to the opportunities of higher education. We would not be faced with the critical problems of urban renewal if ours were not a highly mobile society, both economically and geographically; stable communities, such as those in Europe, have much less difficulty in maintaining their cities. We have racial problems precisely because we are making progress in lowering racial barriers, and we have political problems because our democratic processes are becoming more pervasive and more deeply rooted. Ours are the problems of growth, not of decay, though they are no less difficult and variegated for that. Because they are problems of growth they are susceptible of creative solutions, even though the solutions themselves will unquestionably pose new problems which will call for continued creativity at perhaps even higher levels. This, in Toynbee's terms, is the distinctive characteristic of a society in growth.

If growth is to be maintained, the society must find effective solutions to each successive major problem as it arises. The price of failure is breakdown, initially in restricted areas but eventually for the society as a whole, for failure in one area is likely to inhibit the problem-solving process in other areas. Thus the problems of education, of race relations, and of urban blight and decay, while conceptually distinct, are intimately related, and failure in any one area will heavily compromise the others.

Responsibility for dealing with such problems rests largely with the leadership groups of the society, for they are the only groups possessing the required resources and in a position to act effectively. Businessmen constitute one such group; in contemporary American life they are among the most powerful. They command tremendous economic resources. Their day-to-day business decisions determine the course and character of economic life and of much else besides. Probably to a greater extent than in any previous society, the American businessman exercises a profound influence on his life and times. Such power carries with it a commensurate responsibility.

The businessman's responsibility is not confined to his own enterprise. For one thing, he is a citizen as well as a businessman, and as a citizen he has a stake in the society as a whole. As a businessman he has a similar stake. No business is an island, and the business system is not an island; the system and the individual enterprise owe their character to the society in which they have their being, and their future is intimately bound up with the future of that society. In a strict sense the corporation is not a citizen, but it has many citizen-like attributes. It has rights and responsibilities that are mutually dependent and which are not obscured or essentially altered by the fact of corporate rather than individual personality. In many ways the obligations of the corporate citizen are more far-reaching than those of individual citizens simply because of the corporation's greater resources of money and manpower. For these reasons the businessman must give cognizance to many affairs not traditionally considered matters of business concern.

The area of the businessman's responsibility is not unbounded. Businessmen cannot deal, either individually or collectively, with all the problems of contemporary American society. But they can deal with problems which though not strictly business in nature have a demonstrable relationship to the business system and to the solution of which their position and experience as businessmen enable them to contribute effectively. Interest and competence thus respresent a twofold principle of selection for determining the areas in which businessmen can work with propriety and hope of accomplishment.

Some problems are more intimately related to business than others. Education, for example, is a matter of prime importance to the economic life of the nation. Music and the arts, essential as they may be to the cultural health and the spiritual well-being of the society, are less business-connected. The businessman *as a businessman* can appropriately interest himself in many of the problems of education. *As an individual,* he may also interest himself in music and the arts and devote much of his time and resources to their encouragement, but the connection between such interests and his business interests is likely to be tenuous.

II

There are two chief avenues for the exercise of corporate citizenship: philanthropic giving and personal participation.

The philanthropic businessman is not a new phenomenon in American society. Historically, men of wealth have frequently devoted large parts of their fortunes to a variety of charitable purposes. Within this generation, however, there has been a revolutionary change in the American tax structure. Great fortunes accumulated in the past are now materially depleted by inheritance taxes; the accumulation of new fortunes has been seriously impeded by steeply progressive income taxes. Modern systems of taxation have relegated the large private donor to a secondary role. It is logical that industry step into this breach and assume its share of the burden. In a sense the mantle of the large private donor has fallen to the corporation.

The legal groundwork for corporate giving was laid less than twenty-five years ago when corporate tax laws were amended to permit tax-exempt deductions up to 5 per cent of net corporate income. Until after World War II, corporate giving was largely restricted to local welfare causes, such as community funds, and to a few national causes, such as the Red Cross and the United Service Organizations, which were closely associated with the war effort. During the past ten years, however, there has been a great proliferation in corporate giving, both in total volume and in variety of causes supported. This trend is attributable to a number of factors, among the most important of which is the growing sense of public responsibility on the part of the managers of corporate enterprise.

Today the responsibility of the corporation to contribute to the financial support of civic activities is well recognized. Hospitals, social agencies, welfare and charitable organizations of many kinds depend on business for a major share of their support. Corporate aid to education is becoming of increasing importance to the survival and growth of the private, independent colleges and universities. In many other fields the financial support of business is essential to the maintenance of services on which the American community has come to depend.

There are important differences between personal and corporate philanthropy. The individual of means has wide latitude in the disposal of his personal fortune. He can endow a college or build a church or support an orphanage, as his private inclinations dictate. Within limits, he need not concern himself with what the public or his business associates or his customers think; the money is his and he can do with it as he chooses. When the manager of a broadly owned corporation makes decisions on giving, however, the money is not his own but the corporation's. It is money which essentially is held in trust and must be administered accordingly. Because charitable contributions are tax-exempt, they are in a sense public moneys and must be handled with due regard to the public interest. And because the total volume of corporate giving has grown so great, the corporate manager must take into account its total impact on the community. No longer can he dispense funds according to his own personal likes and dislikes. No doubt personal tastes play an important part in what actually happens, but even the most prejudiced manager will always seek a rationale for his decisions that in some way relates the giving not only to the needs of the community but to the needs and interests of the corporation. Implicit is the recognition that corporate giving reflects the corporation and not the individual, and that it must therefore be an expression of corporate policy and not of individual whim.

The resources of any corporation are necessarily limited, in manpower as well as money; it cannot participate in or aid in the support of all the causes that may lay claim to its interests. By doing what it is fitted to do, by avoiding what it cannot do well or what others can do better, the corporation's resources are used to best advantage.

From the standpoint of the corporation, the search for rationality helps emphasize the public character of its actions, which is a salutary discipline for its managers. From the standpoint of the community, it provides a somewhat more orderly assessment of community needs and a somewhat better balanced distribution of philanthropic resources. These are clear gains.

The quest for rationality, however, carries with it certain dangers. There is the danger, for example, that the pervasiveness of the self-interest concept in economic affairs may tend to restrict unduly the range and character of causes which the corporation's managers feel justified in supporting. In many cases the effort is made to equate philanthropy to the profit and loss statement, however tenuous and labored the connection. This makes sense only if the role of the corporation is conceived in the narrow terms of traditional laissez-faire economics. What is needed is a broad conception of the role of the modern corporation as an instrumentality of public service, with many interests in mutuality with various segments of the larger society.

A company's obligation to the community cannot, however, be discharged solely through financial contributions. Financial support is important, but perhaps the easiest form of corporate responsibility to fulfill. Much more important and demanding is the personal involvement of the corporation's officers, executives, and employees in the significant affairs of their community. If financial support were all that were involved, an argument could be made for replacing it with tax money, which would spread the burden more equitably among all corporations and provide a more assured source of income for needed community services. But tax money cannot substitute for the voluntary efforts of responsible citizens.

The businessman has certain important competencies for dealing with civic problems by virtue of his position, experience, and skills as a businessman. His stature in the community and his established relationships with leaders in varied walks of life are of some consequence in furthering the causes he elects to foster. More important, his experience in the business world often enables him to bring to such causes a viewpoint and an understanding of great value to their successful prosecution. His knowledge of finance, of organization, of practical administration are especially useful, as are the drive and determination with which he is accustomed to pursue his business affairs. These qualities supplement the technical skills and training of the professionals in the various areas in which he chooses to operate.

One of the greatest assets the businessman can bring to such causes is his skill and experience in leadership. The business world exercises so strong an attraction in our society that a large part of the leadership talent, which in other times and other societies has been drawn to other fields, in our time and in our country finds its way into business and industry. If that talent does not make itself available in some measure to other than business affairs (narrowly defined), other areas are likely to be deprived of the leadership they need. This is not to assert that business has a monopoly or near-monopoly on leadership skills, but rather to suggest that since such skills are relatively scarce, some portion of those which may be lodged in the business community should be made available to other causes.

Not the least of the assets the businessman brings to civic affairs is his long perspective. Especially if his business experience has been acquired in a large, publicly owned corporation, he is accustomed to thinking in relatively long time spans rather than primarily in terms of immediate issues and immediate problems. By the same token, he is used to initiating action which may not show tangible results for years. The value of this can be seen, for example, in dealing with the consequences of urban blight and decay and in developing programs for urban renewal. By their very nature, problems such as these cannot be worked out quickly; long-range plans must be developed which may require a generation or more for successful accomplishment. The habit of mind acquired in managing the affairs of a corporation which presumably will long outlive its present managers is especially valuable for this purpose, and it is no accident that businessmen are playing a central role in the many efforts now under way to improve the American city as a place to live and work.

Competencies such as these are essential for many civic undertakings. The businessman who gives money without giving himself short-changes his community. He short-changes himself as well, because his money is less effective and produces a lesser result.

III

The businessman giving thought as a businessman to the problems of his community is responding to a deeply ingrained tradition of American life: the tradition of voluntary citizen action on matters of common concern. Essentially this is an extension of the principle of personal responsibility. Typically, this principle expresses itself through the medium of voluntary civic associations.

The American people from their earliest history have displayed a genius for organization, much of it essentially spontaneous. Tocqueville noted this characteristic more than a century ago, and other foreign observers have commented on it frequently, sometimes with amusement but always with wonder. We are a nation of joiners, and more than one commentator has noted that no problem can exist for long in this country without some kind of society being set up to deal with it.

Thus we have organizations to serve a wide variety of charitable purposes, to promote education, to prevent cruelty to animals, to encourage international understanding, to protect minority interests, to foster trade and commerce, to secure specific legislation, to improve housing conditions, to encourage better farming, to protect natural resources, to enforce professional ethics—and so on. We even have associations of associations, and—especially significant for their symbolic content—voluntary associations of formal governmental bodies, as for example the Council of State Governments. We are indeed a nation of organizers; therein lies much of our strength and vitality.

There are good historical reasons for this strong propensity of Americans to set up voluntary organizations to serve practically every conceivable purpose. The development of American society has always outrun government. In colonial days and on the frontier, the citizen was largely on his own. If he had problems of providing a livelihood, building a house, settling a community, protecting himself from the Indians, or dealing with unexpected disaster, he had nowhere to turn but to himself and to his fellows. Problems which in older societies, as in Europe, led men to look to government for relief, or to the church or the lord of the manor, had to be dealt with, if they were dealt with at all, by the informal, voluntary, largely spontaneous, cooperation of the citizens themselves.

Great as has been the extension of the scope of government in recent years, it has fallen far short of the phenomenal growth of American society. In terms of the problems faced by the people of this country in the complex life of today, government is still rudimentary, still poorly adapted to deal with any but the broadest, the most abstract, and in a sense the simplest of issues. For most of the problems of living, the citizen is still on his own. And because the individual citizen is still weak and his personal resources still limited, he still turns instinctively, as his forefathers did, to voluntary co-operation with like-minded and like-problemed fellow citizens. This tendency has not been weakened by the rich and prolific growth of religious organizations during the last hundred years, nor by the phenomenal development of the modern corporation, which has taken over some of the same kind of social service functions once performed by the medieval city. The individual citizen works with and through his church and his company much as he works with and through the many other voluntary organizations he has created to help serve the many purposes he demands be served.

We cannot understand our democracy without understanding the richness and vitality of our system of informal, private citizen associations. Such organizations are one of the important means by which individuals can assume and exercise the responsibilities of citizenship in a democracy. For democracy demands responsibility—not some vague, ill-defined, abstract responsibility, but concrete, specific, continuing responsibility for the day-to-day affairs of society. The importance of the private, voluntary association consists in large part in the fact that it provides the means by which individual citizens can recognize and discharge that kind of responsibility.

Thus the businessman, when he takes account of problems

beyond the corporate bounds of his own enterprise, turns instinctively to some form of voluntary civic organization. This may be a trade association, or a welfare group, or a political party, or a community improvement organization, or a planning council, or any number of other temporary or permanent organizations of citizens with a common interest in specified areas. They are the primary means through which the businessman exercises his responsibilities as a citizen, and they provide much of the mechanism through which he is able to act effectively.

In a sense, the system of voluntary civic associations is an application of the principle of free enterprise. More accurately, the corporation itself is a special type of voluntary association: a group of citizens freely associated to serve needs that can only be served in concert. In the case of the corporation these needs are primarily economic. For the many needs other than economic and outside the corporation which must likewise be served, the normal mode of action is the civic association. In both cases drive and direction come not from a central locus of authority but from many centers of initiative. Free, private economic institutions and voluntary, private citizen associations thus comprise a common system; neither could long exist without the other.

IV

In the absence of business support—in money as well as manpower—many of the activities now conducted on a private basis would perforce have to be taken over by government. This would, of course, increase the cost of government, and business and businessmen would have to bear a major part of the higher tax burden. Money costs aside, many needs cannot be as well served by government as by private agencies. Even under a federal system, government tends toward the monolithic. Private efforts are more efficient, more flexible, more responsive to changing needs and circumstances, more experimental, more inclined to explore alternatives; private undertakings are characterized by more diversity, more independence, more originality—and more humanity. These are attributes of a pluralistic society.

The personal participation of a company's officers and executives in important civic affairs—generally through the medium of organized groups—helps promote close, harmonious, and cooperative relationships between the company and major segments of the social structure. Apart from the intrinsic value of such activities and apart from their impact on the community, they provide a means whereby the company can be accepted as a corporate citizen and its people recognized for their skill, their competence, their leadership qualities, and their integrity and good will. Through support of programs concerned with vital civic problems, corporate management can demonstrate in a tangible and recognizable way its concern for the welfare of the community, and in so doing say to the people of the community something it could never say to them in words. This is one of the significant ways the businessman can help make business meaningful to society.

Education for Business Leadership

I

The responsibilities of the modern businessman are broader, his duties more complex than they are often conceived to be. How well are people being prepared for careers in today's business world—in particular, for careers that will lead to the higher policy-making positions? Without suggesting that college training is necessarily a prerequisite for such positions, and recognizing that people rise into the leadership ranks from many different types of college backgrounds, it is nevertheless appropriate in the present context to examine the kind and quality of education provided by the collegiate schools of business, the one sector of our system of higher education specifically committed to education for business.

A strong argument can be made that effective performance in any line of endeavor requires not only mastery of a specific body of information and techniques but a basic understanding of the traditions and values of one's society and a working knowledge of the structure and dynamics of that society. Without the latter, skill in technique and mastery of specific knowledge may lead to aimless and barren effort. Without the former, immersion in traditions and values and verbal mastery of concepts are likely to lead to dilettantism. Effective discharge of the responsibilities of citizenship requires specific knowledge and skills directed and controlled in terms of basic values and in line with the requirements and opportunities of contemporary society. The weight and importance of both these broad areas have increased significantly in the last couple of generations.

Time was when the task of learning to be a farmer or a businessman—or, for that matter, a lawyer or engineer or doctor—was relatively simple. A few years of exposure and practice were all that were necessary, assuming basic competence and a reasonable measure of luck, to achieve high levels of performance. The youthful age at which John D. Rockefeller, Andrew Carnegie, and the Guggenheim sons achieved phenomenal success is evidence of the rapidity with which the essential facts and skills of business could be mastered in an earlier and simpler day.

The task of achieving success in any line of endeavor is far more difficult today. In part, this is a result of increasing rigidities in our society, and particularly of the fact that advancement is more and more dependent on progress through established organizational hierarchies with fewer opportunities for brilliant independent improvisation. But it is also and more importantly a result of the increasing complexity of skills necessary for economic success and the rapidly growing body of knowledge required for intelligent economic activity.

At the same time, basic grounding in the values and traditions of democratic American life and understanding of the functioning of modern society have not decreased in importance. Indeed, with the growing interdependence of economic life and the ever-increasing burdens laid upon the businessman for the maintenance of the material—and, in many respects, the ethical and spiritual—base of our society, these considerations assume far greater importance than they did in the past.

There are too few schools of business that conceive the task of educating businessmen in such terms. A common failing is undue specialization and undue emphasis on techniques. Many schools do a fairly good job of developing staff and technical people but seldom top people. They are good at teaching business methods but not at preparing men for leadership. They produce many "experts" but few "statesmen." In part, this stems from the difficulty of determining what to teach and how. The problem of curriculum planning is real. It is far easier to develop a course in, say, credit management or personnel or time and motion study, than to develop one dealing with the nature of the enterprise.

Business itself must bear a considerable part of the responsibility for the schools' failure on this point. Business organizations have become so systematized and specialized that much of their demand is for people who have been trained in specific techniques or who can fit readily into specialized compartments of the business structure. Training of this kind often meets the immediate needs of business, but its long-range value is questionable. It may serve to get men off to a quick start, but it is likely to limit them later on. Many schools give the impression of having followed too slavishly the expressed desires of business without exercising real leadership themselves. Because often their chief contacts have been not so much with genuine business leaders as with staff specialists, the schools have received a somewhat distorted picture of the real nature and the real needs of business.

The relationship of the schools of business to business is different from the relationship of the schools of medicine and law to their respective professions. Professional schools such as these do far more than merely prepare newcomers for entry into particular careers; they provide active leadership to the professions themselves. They establish standards, synthesize experience, formulate principle. They endeavor not only to keep abreast of developments within their respective professions but also to keep ahead of them. Business is sorely in need of similar leadership from the schools of business.

The proper function of the schools of business should be conceived as developing the future members of one of the key leadership groups of modern American society. This will require a program that seeks to impart the fundamental values of a free society: a program that will inculcate a better understanding of that society and the forces at work within it; a program that will help the businessman understand his place in the scheme of things and his responsibility to the whole; and, above all, a program that will emphasize the crucial responsibilities of leadership, because only through understanding and accepting—and effectively executing—its responsibilities can any leadership group long survive.

II

What is chiefly required is a conception of the primary function of business education as preparation for social and not merely technical leadership and the development of curricula and faculties that will adequately support that conception. Certain crucial areas in such curricula may be suggested.

There is, for example, the problem of change. If our free society is to survive, it must continue to change, because change is the essence of its being. The schools of business, however, do little to prepare businessmen to understand the changes going on around them or to accept change as an essential characteristic of the American way of life. On the contrary, the schools tend to emphasize the static and in so doing confirm and strengthen the social prejudices of their students. This has aggravated the sometimes marked unwillingness of businessmen to explore means for dealing with problems as they arise.

This is a dangerous position; one measure of its danger is the extent to which business lost out during the 1930's and 1940's in the struggle for political power. As members of a leadership group, businessmen must assist in developing policies that will deal effectively with emerging problems, many of which are created by advances within business itself. Not to do so, or merely to resist change, is to abdicate and through default allow others to exercise the initiative. If the schools of business are to serve their proper function, they must deal realistically with the problem of change.

One aspect of the tendency among schools of business to emphasize the static rather than the dynamic aspects of business and society is their failure to appreciate the importance of history. Here again the schools have followed the lead of business itself. American businessmen as a group display remarkably little sense of history—at least so far as business is concerned. What is needed is not preoccupation with the past but an understanding of how the present evolved out of the past and how the future is in process of evolving out of the present. The businessman needs an acute sense of where business is going, and he cannot have that in proper degree without knowing where it has been. The study and teaching of business history as distinct from economic and social history is a comparatively recent and still restricted development. This is a critical failure of many schools of business.

By and large business has not fared too well at the hands of the historians. This is not to deny that business has made mistakes which should properly be recorded as history. But many businessmen reading historical accounts in later years of events in which they had a part have difficulty in understanding the interpretation placed upon them, and sometimes even in identifying the events themselves. This is in part due to the fact that business has left so inadequate a record of its own actions and its own evaluation of the context in which such actions occurred.

The history of labor relations is a case in point. By far the largest bodies of data available to historians of labor relations are the records of unions, the recollections of labor leaders, and the observations of outside parties; there is little documentary evidence on the business side. This imbalance continues to exist in the documentation of current labor history. When the labor history of the current period comes to be written, it will be distorted because the basic documentary record is distorted—not because anyone has schemed it so, but because business and its representatives are so deficient in their sense of history.

Generally speaking, the schools of business have taken little interest in labor unions or in union-management relations. They have many courses in "personnel"—hiring, record keeping, training, and the like—but they have tended to steer clear of the touchy matters of unionism. And yet there are few subjects of more importance to the prospective businessman than the history, characteristics, and aspirations of the labor movement.

The schools of business are ideally situated to take the lead in expanding the study of business history, as some of them are already doing to good effect. Such leadership will not only serve important scholarly purposes but can be a means of developing a better feeling for and understanding of the place of business in an evolving historical milieu on the part of those who one day will be part of that history themselves.

III

The schools of business must achieve a closer integration with business itself. Two avenues are available—among others —which should be especially useful for this purpose. These are: (1) the further development of instructional programs for people already holding responsible positions in business and (2) the development of more vigorous and more creative research.

There is growing concern today that many of the business schools are missing what well might be their most important "student body," and a growing conviction that more of their efforts might be properly directed toward serving the needs of people already in business and hence in a position to assimilate and utilize the instruction the schools (potentially at least) are uniquely qualified to give. This is not to minimize the importance of business education at the graduate and undergraduate levels; there are great and vital needs in this area that must be served. Adequate preparation for the role of the modern businessmen, however, can scarcely be acquired in the four short years of college or one or two years of graduate school; a lifetime, indeed, is none too long. Theoretical considerations aside, we are forced by the facts of contemporary life to a concept of *continuing* education, a concept which visualizes the individual as learning and growing far beyond the customary limits of studenthood and well into and beyond the years of peak economic achievement.

Students who have had no experience in the world of business are poorly equipped for instruction in the methods of business. They do not have the background of information and understanding necessary to give meaning and significance to what they are taught. Much of the learning is rote; particularly where it is in terms of specific practices, rather than principles, it is likely to be of little value because of the diversities between business enterprises and because the rapidity of change in the business world renders many practices out of date before the ink is dry on the textbooks describing them.

To a considerable extent, the specific knowledge and techniques of business can best be learned in actual experience on the job. There is, however, a growing need for instruction supplementary to job experience. As each business specialty has become increasingly involved, more time and effort is required to learn it—a process which can be greatly facilitated by proper off-the-job instruction. Moreover, because of the greater time required for proficiency in each specialization, opportunities for acquiring a breadth of experience are becoming increasingly limited. Here, too, off-the-job instruction can serve a useful purpose. Above all, a creatively conceived program of continuing education can assist not only in imparting knowledge of specific practices and techniques, but in giving the searching student a better understanding of his own experiences and a better appreciation of the problems of the business as a whole.

To develop the kind of men industry needs today, it is not enough to take young college graduates and immerse them in the business world, assuming that learning and growth will automatically follow. Executive development must be seen as a perpetual learning process, both within and outside the company. And the executive of the future may well be a man whose pursuit of knowledge and understanding continues all his life.

Adult business education can be particularly valuable to companies which adhere to the practice of promotion from within. The development of executives within a company has many values, from the standpoint both of good human relations and of gearing developmental activities to company needs. But promotion from within has one serious shortcoming: the tendency toward provincialism, toward narrowness of outlook and perspective. Furthermore, in companies offering substantial, long-range promotional opportunities people with humble beginnings often progress quite far up the ladder only to find their further progress blocked by limited education. In both these matters, effective facilities for adult business education can render important services.

Progressive business managements are coming more and more to realize the values of continuing education and are making increasing demands on established educational institutions in this respect. In response to these demands, a number of encouraging experiments are already under way. Noteworthy are the executive program of the University of Chicago, the Sloan fellowships at the Massachusetts Institute of Technology, and the advanced management program at Harvard. Experiments such as these are the most significant development in business education since the inception of the business school idea toward the end of the last century.

Over and above the values of adult business education per se, programs for executives can be useful as a means for integrating the work of the schools more closely with the realities of business. Furthermore, such programs can serve as channels of communication to the business community that will assist the schools in exerting the influence and the leadership that, as professional schools, they should provide.

IV

Research represents a further means for the exercise of professional leadership. The schools of business should be constantly studying the problems of business and doing so in meaningful and creative ways. The results of such research should be used to enrich the content of business courses and should be communicated by a variety of means to the business community. The example of the schools of medicine suggests the vital relation of research to leadership.

Much of the business research now being conducted, however, is limited in concept and inept in method. It deals largely with the description of procedures or the tabulation of practices and only rarely involves ideas or problems of more than incidental significance. One suspects that the aridity of these efforts reflects lack of understanding on the part of many business-school faculties as to the real nature and problems of business. It also reflects a lack of knowledge of the progress which has been made in the social sciences during the last quarter century. Much of the thinking of the schools of business still rests implicitly on the work of Herbert Spencer. There have been tremendous developments in psychology, sociology, and anthropology which are potentially of great significance to business, but few schools of business seem to be aware of them.

There should be attractive opportunities for cooperation in research between the various social sciences and the schools of business. For one thing, large sums of money are being expended for research in the social science field, and the business schools are missing what could be an excellent financial advantage. But they are missing far more than this in failing to channel a larger portion of the total research efforts of the universities into areas of importance not only to business as such but to the community at large. Above all, they are missing the opportunity of enriching their own knowledge of the fundamental problems of man and society, which are the proper concern of institutions charged with responsibility for educating present and future businessmen.

More active cooperation in research between the schools of business and other branches of the universities can also serve an important function for higher education in general. One of the great challenges of modern education is the need for effective integration among the various specialized disciplines. The bodies of knowledge in the various fields have grown so vast and so complex and at the same time so interrelated that cross-fertilization of ideas is increasingly necessary. The schools of business are in a position to assist in meeting this challenge. Business by its very nature has to deal with the subject matter of many different specialties as a totality. This special role of business should offer attractive possibilities for close integration, through the schools of business, of a wide variety of disciplines. Integration in this manner would also serve to keep research realistically oriented toward action. Not the least benefit of such a course would be a vast enrichment of business scholarship and a considerable enhancement of the professional status and leadership potential of the business schools themselves.

Imaginative and creative research can also be an important means for integrating the schools of business more closely with the business community. American business is singularly research-minded, and cooperation is likely to be readily forthcoming, provided the research projects are properly conceived and provided the business community has sufficient confidence in and respect for the institution sponsoring the research.

Businessmen, understandably, tend to be more interested in "practical" than in so-called "pure" research. But the importance of pure research in the physical sciences has been demonstrated so dramatically in recent years, and so many industrial research laboratories are devoting portions of their staffs and budgets to pure-research purposes, that appeals for support from the field of business should not fall on deaf ears. The conceptual framework within which most schools of business operate is, however, still in such a rudimentary stage that it is scarcely possible to visualize either the subject matter or the methodology of pure research in business. Until this limitation is overcome, it is useless to talk of the possibilities of anything but applied research. But applied research properly conceived and executed and its findings imaginatively evaluated can itself be the means for constructing the conceptual framework within which pure research can become possible. And pure research, in turn, can inform and guide applied research into more creative and constructive channels.

V

Education—whether business or otherwise—is concerned with ideas. Any leadership group must be concerned with "great ideas." One of the essential functions of institutions charged with the preparation of members of leadership groups must be the refinement and elaboration and the effective communication of the great ideas which guide those groups.

Several ideas underlie American business, ideas that set it off sharply from European business. There is, for example, the idea of management itself, a special group within the enterprise which is carefully chosen for its competence and responsibility for the success of the enterprise. This is a far cry from the typical European enterprise, which is likely to be controlled by absentee owners but actually run by clerks and technicians. There is the idea that business exists for purposes broader than merely earning dividends for absentee owners; that the rewards of increased productivity must be shared with customers in the form of lower prices and with workers in the form of higher wages; that an adequate portion of profits must be utilized for such essentially social purposes as improvement of facilities and equipment.

There is the idea that business is *accountable* (i.e., "answerable") for its stewardship not only to stockholders but to customers, employees, and the public. There is the idea of the "mass" rather than the "class" market, and, closely related, the idea that markets are not static but are subject to practically indefinite expansion—that business through competition creates markets and that competition broadens the market for all. The cartel system has never taken hold in this country in any important way simply because it is uncongenial to an environment permeated with ideas such as these.

There is the idea that diversity and experimentation are "good" in themselves because they reflect and express the spontaneity which is so basic an ingredient of American life and character. There is the idea that all relations with employees must be based on respect for human beings—not human beings in a hypothetical mass but concrete, individual men and women—the idea that people must be treated not merely as means but as ends in themselves.

These are "great ideas," ideas that are essentially ethical in nature and that spring ultimately from the Judeo-Christian tradition as enriched and unfolded by the special circumstances of American history. It is ideas such as these, and the ethical tradition they express, that, more than any other factor—more than our tremendous natural resources, more than our vast free market, more than our mechanical and inventive ingenuity—account for the economic progress this country has enjoyed.

The definition, elaboration, and refinement of the "great ideas" of American business and the communication of these ideas to the rising generation of businessmen represent the most important task ahead for the schools of business.

Chapter ELEVEN

The Businessman and Government

I

American businessmen as a group have not exhibited marked skill in the arts of government and political affairs. This is a curious condition to find among a social and economic elite which has shown such pronounced capacities for leadership in other fields.

A basic factor is the businessman's traditional distrust of government, which arises in considerable part from his fondness for laissez-faire economics. Government is likely to be considered at best a necessary evil, and the less government the better. The fact that business has long since discarded much of laissez-faire in its practice has not materially weakened it as an ideal; nowhere is this clearer than in the businessman's concept of what should be the relationship between business and government. Nor is this concept seriously modified by the readiness with which he turns to government for aid when it suits his own purposes. Actually the businessman, in common with his fellow Americans of all classes, looks on government as a service to be commanded as needed, but this has not greatly changed his conviction that government should be kept within strict bounds, particularly as far as his own business is concerned.

In all justice, the businessman has cause for distrusting the growth of government and its encroachment on business affairs. Businessmen bear a heavy portion of the tax load of the country through the corporate income tax and the graduated personal income tax. Each increase in the size of government and in the level of government expenditures is a matter of direct concern to the businessman, and he may be pardoned an inclination to question their necessity when he pays so large a part of the cost. He is not merely concerned over loss of personal income; more important, he is disturbed over the effect of tax policies on economic growth. Nor is he reassured by what might be called the "ratchet effect" of government expenditures, whereby increases are usually met by raising corporate and personal income taxes but curtailments are seldom accompanied by corresponding cuts.

The amount of record keeping that is necessary for government purposes is great—and expensive. Frequently the businessman is severely limited in his freedom of action by governmental restrictions. Unquestionably, much of the experience businessmen have with government is painful: struggling with red tape, avoiding legal infringements, arguing with regulatory agencies, contesting undesired legislation, defending business actions before courts of law or investigating committees, and in myriad other ways seeking protection against threats and harassments of government origin. It is little wonder that the typical businessman expresses a strong preference for the idea of limited government and that his experience with big government leaves him with distrust.

This distrust is reinforced by a skeptical attitude toward politics in general. To the typical businessman, politics, if not exactly a dirty word, often carries an unsavory connotation with overtones suggesting graft and corruption or at least their ever-present possibility. Politics, moreover, are "messy." The businessman is accustomed to efficiency, clear lines of authority, orderly division of labor, precise definitions of relationships between functions and groups, unambiguous centers of responsibility. These he does not find in the political arena. There is a tendency to view politicians in terms of gross caricature: as windy characters not too heavily burdened by principle, not given overmuch to veracity, and not exactly the kind of people a businessman would want to seek out for boon companionship. Government, in a word, is likely to be suspect because there are so many politicians in it.

Other factors besides skepticism have militated against the businessman's taking an active part in political affairs. Perhaps the most important of these is lack of time. There may be a growing problem of leisure in our society, but it is not a problem of the businessman. In an age of the five-day forty-hour week for rank-and-file employees, and predictions of still shorter working hours in the foreseeable future, the businessman continues to work almost unlimited hours. This raises an interesting speculation. In the history of most civilizations political power has gravitated to the class which has the leisure to cultivate the political arts. In America today the group with the greatest amount of leisure is the working class. It is perhaps no accident, nor merely the result of Walter Reuther's prodding, that organized labor is playing an increasingly active role in political affairs; it may be in large part a consequence of a tendency on the part of groups with well-defined economic interests and blessed with leisure time to turn spontaneously to politics and government.

II

The businessman's reluctance to become involved in politics, and the difficulties in the way of his becoming involved, have had serious consequences. He has a vital stake in both politics and government, not only as a businessman but as a citizen; politics and government for their part have great need for the skills and experience he can bring to them. If they are not all the businessman would like them to be, the blame rests in part with the businessmen themselves because of their aloofness from political and governmental affairs.

But above all, the failure of businessmen as a group to play an active political role places business in a vulnerable position. This is not merely because political leadership is left to drift by default into the hands of other groups who may not be sympathetic to the needs of business and who in the pursuit of their own aims may impose burdens and restrictions that seriously hamper business in the performance of its economic and social functions. Even more dangerous is the fact that failure to participate actively in the political life of the country tends to make businessmen as a group unduly naïve about political processes. This lack of understanding and consequent lack of skill places business at a grave disadvantage. More than that, it represents a serious flaw in the workings of our democratic social order; for a democracy requires a high degree of political skill in all groups which comprise the society.

The recurring emphasis in the thinking of businessmen on the nonproductive role of government makes it difficult for them to understand or appreciate the essential services provided by government and creates a tendency to look on all government functions as parasitical. This attitude has on occasion led business groups into bizarre behavior. A case in point is the vociferous budget-cutting drive in the spring of 1957. Granted that the President had presented to Congress the largest peacetime budget in the country's history and granted the need for careful scrutiny of many of its provisions, the fact remains that the manner in which powerful business groups attacked the budget seriously weakened the position of a President generally considered favorably disposed toward business. Undoubtedly many of those most active in the drive supported the election of President Eisenhower, but few of them apparently realized the extent to which they were destroying public confidence in his administration and thus increasing the likelihood of a change in party control in 1960.

The fact that businessmen as perhaps the strongest single group backing the President displayed so little political wisdom—and so little loyalty—was not lost on political leaders, who may be inclined to look elsewhere in the future for the stable and reliable support needed to carry forward a successful party program. The practical politician is above all practical. His success depends on the sureness of his judgment in assessing his sources of support and the issues that will mobilize that support. His confidence in business must have been severely shaken. By contrast, he is likely to be impressed with the greater political skill and loyalty of organized labor. Labor no less than business has frequently been disappointed by parties and administrations. But in its disappointment on specific matters it has not lashed out in such a way as to undermine those on whom it depends for general support of its program. Organized labor in this sense shows much more political realism than organized business.

Because of his reluctance to become personally engaged in political affairs, and his sense of unsureness when he does, the businessman tends to look to trade associations not only for guidance on political questions but to carry the brunt of political action on behalf of business. Whatever advantages this approach may have, it has several serious weaknesses. The need for consensus to empower a trade association to act is likely to mean that on any particular issue the association's position will represent a kind of "least common denominator" of ideas, which is seldom striking for its imaginativeness or originality and may not be really responsive to the problem at hand.

Trade association policy positions moreover, are more frequently negative than positive, opposing rather than proposing, simply because it is easier to obtain consensus in the face of threats than in the face of opportunities. For this reason much of the political activity on behalf of business is defensive, the fighting of rear-guard actions. Business and its trade associations generally have a considerable measure of success in opposition. At any given session of Congress, for example, most of the legislative proposals to which business objects can count on defeat. But some almost always slip through, with the net result that over a series of sessions a fairly considerable body of legislation is enacted which businessmen feel is inimical to the interests of business and of the economy. Business would be in a much stronger position if it were more often *for* things rather than everlastingly *against*. Business would appear more favorably in the public eye if it took more initiative in devising measures for dealing with urgent public problems. By allowing the initiative to pass to others business allows problems to be defined in *their* terms and permits the issues to be debated on *their* grounds. The best that business can hope for under these circumstances is compromise or delay.

Businessmen would be well advised to rely less on their trade associations for political purposes and more on their own resources, less on formal statements of policy positions and more on their own independent evaluation of issues and possible alternative courses of action. Business needs articulate spokesmen who know how to express its real interests and the relation of those interests to community and national needs. There will always be an important place for the trade association, but there is no substitute for independent thinking and action on the part of individual businessmen who are willing to keep themselves adequately informed and who, when they take a position or voice an opinion, can be listened to with respect.

IV

A major reason for the lack of skill of business in the conduct of its political affairs is lack of experience in practical politics. The businessman almost never seeks elective office, and while he may occasionally accept an appointive position he does so reluctantly and with keen feelings of self-sacrifice. This is in sharp contrast to the behavior of those with a well-developed political sense who are willing to make an effective commitment to political responsibility and if necessary to claw their way to positions of political power. Power may not always go to those who seek it, but it seldom goes to those who try to avoid it. If business is to strengthen its political position, more individual businessmen will have to become personally involved in the political life of the nation because ultimately it is the stresses and strains of practical politics that determine the course of government.

Businessmen need not feel diffident in seeking to play an active political role any more than they would expect the leaders of organized labor or organized agriculture to feel diffident. Businessmen have points of view and legitimate interests which need to be as effectively prosecuted as those of any other group. No group, moreover, has a monopoly on concern for the general good, and the general good certainly is not served when business fails to assume its full share of the burdens of political responsibility. This is not merely a matter of assuring business a voice in political councils; more important, it is a matter of bringing to political affairs a strength, an experience, and a body of special skills which can represent an important net addition to the vitality of political processes.

The idea of playing a more active role in politics is becoming increasingly popular in business circles. The United States Chamber of Commerce, the National Association of Manufacturers, and a host of other business organizations are urging their members to throw off their traditional distaste and enter the political arena in earnest. Study groups are being set up to instruct businessmen in the strange and intricate ways of politics, and many individual firms are working on plans to encourage political activity on the part of their management personnel. On its face, all of this is a healthy omen. A word of caution, however, is in order.

For one thing, the movement is growing too fast for the growth to be sound. Politics no less than business calls for skill and experience. There is serious danger that enthusiastic amateurs will make mistakes that will give the whole idea of businessmen in politics a bad name, and perhaps irretrievably compromise the very causes they support.

The businessman's traditional reluctance to engage in politics is due at least in part to strong public reaction against corporate political activity in the past. The frank and unabashed manipulations of big business during the latter part of the nineteenth century and the early years of the twentieth created a profound distrust of mixing business and politics. Reentry into politics will reawaken this distrust. Inevitably, the businessman will make mistakes as he moves into an unfamiliar field. Under the circumstances, these mistakes are bound to be magnified in the public eye and in the eyes of professional politicians. The danger is vastly increased if too many businessmen try to move in too quickly, thus multiplying the mistakes and concentrating them in time. What has started out as a trend of great intrinsic value may sputter out as a short-lived fad or—much worse—seriously alienate business from the community at large.

Another area of potential danger is the issue of partisanship. The immediate impetus for the businessman's growing interest in politics is the great increase in the political activities of organized labor, many of which the businessman sees as inimical not only to business but to sound economic growth. In recent years these activities have been largely concentrated within the Democratic party. The businessman-politician is thus likely to focus his own efforts within the Republican party. This, however, creates a dilemma for he recognizes the strength of the public feeling that, politically, corporations must be neuter and is fearful of adverse customer and public reaction if his company should become too closely identified with either of the major political parties.

Typically, therefore, he tries to follow a path of nonpartisanship. But "nonpartisan politics" is a contradiction in terms. Politics by their nature are partisan and can only be prosecuted effectively through political organizations. The businessman who counsels nonpartisanship is reminiscent of the mother who cautioned her daughter to hang her clothes on a hickory limb but not go near the water. Frequently, no doubt, the trappings of nonpartisanship are simply a façade thrown up in an effort to disguise a wholly partisan interest. Such a façade, however, inhibits the effectiveness of the political effort without providing any real protection against public criticism.

In some cases businessmen are so disillusioned with both parties that their nonpartisanship is real. They therefore seek to support or oppose individual candidates rather than either party as such. This independent approach is more forthright than an assumed nonpartisanship, but it overlooks the central role of the party organization in political life. Candidates run as members of a party organization, and their success depends not only on themselves but on their party. Failure to support the party as well as the candidate handicaps both. The party organization provides continuity and is the only effective vehicle for political effort. Attempts to operate outside the party structure are likely to be wasteful and nonproductive.

We have in this country a strong tradition of political independence. Important as he is, however, the independent plays a passive rather than an active role in American politics; he merely responds to the actions of political organizations and has little to do with determining their policies. If businessmen are to exert a positive influence on political affairs, the role of the independent is not for them. They must keep the independent voter in mind, for he often holds the balance of power, but if they are serious in their political aspirations they will have to commit themselves to party politics.

This raises again the problem of how businessmen can engage in partisan political activity without arousing public distrust. The answer lies essentially in keeping the political concerns of the individual businessman separate and distinct from his business. This is not difficult but requires certain policies and rules of conduct.

Religious activities provide a useful precedent. No one questions the right of the businessman to be active in the church of his choice so long as he does not mix his business and sectarian interests. The customers of a particular company do not think of that company as a Catholic organization merely because its president happens to be a practicing member of that faith. So too with politics. The public will readily accept political involvement on the part of individual businessmen so long as they keep their business out of it and keep their politics out of their business. The public objects—and rightly so—to the involvement of the corporation in partisan political activity (as it is becoming increasingly concerned at the similar involvement of great national unions). The public objects equally to the injection of political considerations in the management of the business, as in giving preferment on a basis of political affiliation. But if religion and business can be kept separate, so can politics and business by the same kind of corporate policies and rules of personal behavior.

Just as the head of a business must not try to influence the religious activities of those in his organization, he must not try to influence their political activities. But there is no reason he should not encourage his subordinates to take an active part in politics, so long as he does not try to influence their choice of party. This might be called a *bipartisan* as distinct from a *nonpartisan* approach. The difference lies in recognizing the need for supporting *both* parties rather than following the route of independence or trying to disguise support for one party by protesting special interest in neither. Under a bipartisan approach the businessman would urge his associates to take a more active part in the parties of their choice—*and mean it.* The key is whether the bipartisanship is genuine or merely a gesture for public relations purposes. A genuine bipartisanship is in fact good public relations as well as good politics; because it encourages company executives to be active in both parties, it keeps the corporation as such from being identified with either.

The problem of the businessman in politics turns out to be not such a serious dilemma after all. He can in all good conscience, and without compromising either his business or the cause he is seeking to serve, take an active part in the affairs of his own party and urge his associates to do likewise, each in the party of his own choice. This need not and should not be merely a prudent façade. It can be intensely partisan provided it is genuinely bipartisan. Such an approach is fully consonant with the essentials of the American party system.

V

The genius of the American political system lies not only in its justly famed constitution; it lies equally in the fact that American political parties traditionally have been based primarily on factors other than economic interest or ideological bent. This is not to deny that from time to time in American history the two parties have differed strongly on specific issues: slavery, tariffs, monetary policy, states rights, and the like. However, at no time have all elements of either party been solidly united behind a particular position and at all times minority elements of one party have been more in agreement with the majority of the opposite party than with the majority of their own party. Moreover, while the preponderant opinion of each party may be united on a specific issue of commanding current importance, there are always many other significant issues before the country on which no such internal consensus obtains. As a result, there have been far greater economic and ideological differences *within* each party than there are *between* them. The strength of the system lies precisely in the fact that each party is itself broadly representative of the American people as a whole in all their variety and diversity.

Under this kind of arrangement, differences between interest groups, economic and otherwise, are worked out in part—often in large part—within the parties rather than in struggles between them. In these internal struggles, the official positions of the parties tend to stabilize somewhere near a hypothetical mid-point. And while the position of the Democratic party may stabilize somewhat to the "left" of the Republican party, in actual fact the two are usually not far apart. In other words, the forces within the parties work powerfully toward composing differences, toward finding solutions acceptable to the largest possible number of interest groups. Such solutions may not always be neat and the process of arriving at them may not always be orderly, but considered as a whole they are reasonably effective.

Because of this peculiarity of the American party system, issues can be debated in terms of their individual merits; precisely because the ideological factors are fuzzy they interpose fewer difficulties to the reaching of agreement. While few groups are likely to be entirely happy with the solution reached for any particular problem, most find some measure of satisfaction and none is seriously or irrevocably alienated. The American party system as we know it is probably the most effective means ever devised for handling the political problems of organized society.

One can sympathize with those who long for parties representing clear-cut ideological distinctions, as for example a "liberal" Democratic party and a "conservative" Republican party. Many people, Americans as well as observers from abroad, are confused at the apparently chaotic nature of American politics. Particularly confusing is the fact that each party embraces such extremes within its own organization that the conservative and liberal wings of each have much more in common with the corresponding groups in the opposite party than they have with each other. A realignment of political forces, assuming it could be brought about, would seem more logical and orderly.

Attractive as such a regrouping might appear, however, it could not be achieved without sacrificing some of the distinctive advantages of the present system. A party orientation along conservative and liberal lines would have the inevitable effect of magnifying differences rather than minimizing them. Internal processes would continue to operate toward composing differences within each party, but because each party embraced opposite halves, so to speak, of the political spectrum the two resulting mid-points would be far removed from each other. And the finding of an effective mid-point between *these* two mid-points would be difficult because all the power of each party would be mobilized to defend its position and impose its point of view. Compromise would be difficult because any point yielded would be an ideological as well as a technical concession.

Under the present system actual legislation is usually accomplished not by one party forcing through a preconceived program but by *ad hoc* alliances across party lines, a fact which greatly strengthens the process of accommodation. Under a conservative-liberal alignment party discipline would become much more important, and the more genuinely conservative or liberal each party became, the stronger the discipline would have to be. Each legislator would no longer be a lawmaker in his own right; rather, he would be a pawn in an ideological struggle whose vote on any one issue would be determined not by his own judgment but by the orders of his party leaders. Block voting, centralized control, and rigid party discipline are the inevitable accompaniments of a party system organized along ideological lines.

Under these circumstances there would be strong pressure to convert the two-party system into a multi-party system, because no two parties can adequately represent all the ideological gradations between the far right and the far left. This tendency can be seen in certain European countries, with results few in this country would care to emulate. In all likelihood, however, we would not follow the European course because of a peculiarity of our Constitutional system: the direct (in fact) election of the President and the inability of any splinter party to capture the White House and control of the administrative machinery of the federal government. The dissident subgroups would thus perforce have to remain within one or the other of the two major parties, though not comfortably or happily.

A reorganization of parties along ideological lines would gravely hinder the task of composing differences between conflicting interest groups. Solutions to major national problems would tend to be in terms of the ideology of the party currently in power. One can visualize the manner in which a Farmer-Labor party might tackle the problems of a depression as compared with the way a revived Liberty League might tackle them. Each party, relieved of moderating influences within its own structure, would tend to take extreme positions and to push through extreme forms of legislation. One result would be to alienate the groups represented by the other party and to split the society into irreconcilable camps; "class warfare" would be a fact. Because the ailenated group was still powerful, it would represent an ever-present threat to the party in control. Organized labor would be a threat to a government largely in the hands of business interests; organized business would be a threat to a government largely in the hands of labor interests. Whichever group happened to be in power, there would be strong temptation to resort to force if its power were challenged. From this it might be only a step to dictatorship.

Sharp ideological differences between the parties would greatly increase business uncertainty. Long-range planning and long-term commitments would be risky because of the possible consequences of future changes in the party in power. Historically, the businessman has been able to contemplate changes in political power with a degree of equanimity—as has the labor leader. If the party of his choice lost control of the government he may not have been too happy but he was not likely to feel that the world had come to an end. He may have had to modify certain of his practices, but these were adaptations within a reasonably narrow range.

Many of the greatest problems that confront the country— for example, foreign policy, defense, and education—are not problems with respect to which people are likely to have different views simply because they are workers or employers, farmers or merchants, or members of any of the other economic groups on which ideological differences are usually based. Even economic issues cut across economic classes, as in the case of foreign trade, when certain groups of workers as well as employers stand to lose or gain from changes in international economic policies. The trouble with ideologies is that they are too simple, too abstract, too superficial, too narrow and constricted to serve as reliable guides for action in the face of the many diverse problems confronting the country.

The argument for a non-ideological party system is emphatically not an argument that the parties stand for nothing. The parties must be concerned first and foremost with providing solutions for the major problems of the society, including leadership in the definition of problems, the formulation of workable programs, and the mobilization of popular support for required courses of action. The need is for approaches that are open-minded, questing, flexible; not doctrinaire, rigid, preconceived; approaches that are many-pronged, based on the exploration of alternatives, focused on facts in all their diversity and complexity, not on slogans or oversimplifications. Approaches such as these are best served by a non-ideological system of party organization.

VI

Unfortunately, we have gone a long way toward undermining the traditional basis of the American two-party system, primarily as a result of the political activity of organized labor.

In earlier years labor's political strategy was summed up in the slogan "reward our friends and punish our enemies." This was essentially the role of the political independent, but it proved too passive for the new type of leadership that emerged with the rise of industrial unionism. These new leaders at one time considered launching a third-party movement, but the futility of such an approach in the light of the peculiar American Presidential system soon became clear, and the reorganization of the Democratic party under Franklin D. Roosevelt opened up a more attractive alternative. From the mid-thirties on, therefore, labor has sought to further its political ambitions by working within the Democratic party and by gradually converting that party (or at least its northern wing) into its own political instrument.

Opinions may differ as to the extent this effort has been successful, but there can be no denying that the influence of organized labor has been exerted preponderantly in favor of Democratic candidates and that many present members of Congress owe their election largely to labor support. Neither is there any denying that in key roll-call votes Congressmen so elected vote much more consistently along lines advocated by organized labor than do Congressmen elected without labor support or in the face of strong labor opposition. The fact that practically all Congressmen supported by labor are Democrats and practically all opposed are Republicans is gradually transforming the basis of organization for *both* parties.

While the Democratic party is becoming increasingly dependent on labor the Republican party is becoming increasingly dependent on business. Finding labor support foreclosed to them, some Republican political leaders choose what appears to be the logical alternative. Seeing what is happening to the Democratic party, businessmen turn more and more to the Republican party in the hope of providing a counterweight to labor's growing political strength. As a result the two parties are coming more and more to differ sharply in basic philosophy and programs.

Without denying the propriety of labor's engaging in aggressive political action, businessmen are rightfully concerned at the growing strength of a special-interest group within the body politic; for the resulting imbalance in our political life can have dangerous consequences. In their efforts to redress the balance, however, it is not enough—it is in fact self-defeating—for businessmen to think only in terms of strengthening the Republican party; they must also think in terms of restoring a balance within the Democratic party itself.

It would be a great mistake if the Republican party should ever become the party of business and the Democratic party the party of labor. There is still time to reverse the trend and restore the party system to its traditional non-ideological basis. If this is to be done those businessmen who are of Democratic persuasion—and there are many such—must begin to play an increasingly active role in the affairs of the Democratic party, and those who are of Republic persuasion must do likewise within the Republican party. Just as it is earnestly to be hoped that business will gain a more effective voice in Democratic councils, so it is to be hoped that labor will gain a more effective voice in Republican councils. And just as it is desirable that the Republican party make greater headway in the South and regain some of its former strength in the great metropolitan centers of the North, so it is desirable that the Democratic party make greater progress in areas hitherto traditionally Republican. As each party grows more truly national and more broadly representative in the interest groups it embraces, so will our political institutions be strengthened in their capacity to serve the interests of all the people.

In this, the responsible businessman can play a major part.

Chapter TWELVE

A Political Philosophy for Business

I

Politically, most businessmen probably consider themselves conservatives. Their notion of conservatism is not too well defined but generally speaking it is seen as the antithesis of liberalism, which is not too well defined either. Businessmen tend to associate with conservatism such ideas as concern for stability, protection of business interests, insistence on fiscal responsibility in government. Liberalism is associated with such ideas as social reform, government intervention in private affairs, and free spending. Conservatism is characterized by such adjectives as sound, businesslike, economical, practical; liberalism by the converse. Implicit in this dichotomy is the notion of liberalism as threatening to values prized by the businessman and conservatism as protecting them.

It is unfortunate that words as important as these should be used so loosely, for the inevitable result is confusion. A man's image of himself is largely made up of words. If the businessman's self-image consists of words that are imprecise he may draw a portrait that is misleading both to others and himself.

This has happened in the case of the careless use of the terms liberal and conservative. Because the businessman identifies himself as a conservative, he commits himself to attitudes which range far afield from what he might initially have had in mind. And because he considers liberalism the antithesis of conservatism, he commits himself to opposition to points of view he might otherwise find congenial.

It is the thesis of this chapter—and implicitly the thesis of this entire book—that the philosophy of liberalism is by and large more natural and comfortable for the modern businessman and better fitted to the needs of his role than the philosophy of conservatism.

In the strict sense, conservatism may be defined as a tendency to resist changes in established traditions and institutions; liberalism, as receptiveness to change. A leading exponent of the conservative point of view thus pinpoints the differences in the mood and bias of the two attitudes:

The Conservative's stated preferences [are] for stability over change, experience over experiment, and self-control over self-expression. . . . His urges are toward aristocracy, the Liberal's toward democracy. He makes peace, the Liberal disturbs it. He likes to look back, the Liberal to look ahead . . . the Conservative's confidence in man, democracy, and progress is far weaker than the Liberal's. . . . The Conservative finds this the best of all possible worlds and is generally content to leave well enough alone. The Liberal thinks the world can stand a lot of improving and can't wait to get on with the job.[1]

If blank spaces were used for the two words, many businessmen undoubtedly would pick the description of the liberal as approaching more nearly their own notion of the kind of per-

[1] Clinton Rossiter, *Conservatism in America* (New York: Alfred A. Knopf, Inc., 1955).

sons they consider themselves to be, at least in their roles as businessmen.

One of the reasons the businessman usually thinks of himself as a conservative—and people generally expect him to be—is that historically the man of property has been conservative. In the past the businessman *was* a man of property and the conservative attitude came to him naturally. The modern businessman has inherited the attitude but not the property. He is likely to be a professional manager with only a relatively small ownership interest in the business he manages.

Moreover, as a manager he is likely to be an innovator. His job, in fact, has been called "the management of change." He has much more stake in the emerging future than in the status quo. He is never content with where he stands but is always pushing for new levels of achievement, new fields of endeavor. He is constantly looking for ways to improve and expand his business. He devotes large sums to research and development, leading to a continuous flow of new products, new methods. His sights are always ahead, and most of his important decisions have to do with things to come. These decisions have a profound effect not only on the course of his own business but on the course of society.

We need look back only a few years to see the startling social and economic transformations brought about by the decisions of businessmen: the growth of new industries and the obsolescence of old; shifts in population induced by industrial developments; changes in production technology with resulting changes in economic organization and composition of the work force. There is no indication that the rate of change is slowing down; on the contrary, it appears to be accelerating. In all this the businessman plays the central role. Whatever else it may be, it is not conservative; in terms of results, "revolutionary" would be more apt.

While the word "conservative" may not apply to the manager's business philosophy, he may still think of himself as conservative in matters external to business or in matters likely to impinge on his business. But this is logically inconsistent. More important, it is seriously dysfunctional. The businessman cannot afford to pursue policies of change within his own business and policies which resist change in the world outside. If his role as a businessman is that of innovator, he needs to pursue social and political policies that will support his innovating. If the consequences of his business actions induce social changes he needs to promote social policies that will facilitate the required social adjustments. To promote change on the one hand and to resist the consequences of change on the other creates needless stress and seriously inhibits the innovating process.

II

A brief survey of areas on which people are likely to take positions characterized as liberal or conservative suggests the consistency with which the liberal position best fits the nature and interests of business.

A free economy is necessarily an unstable economy. It is characterized by ups and downs in over-all levels of activity and employment, and by the rise of new industries and the decline of old. To eliminate fluctuations would require a degree of central control that would totally transform the system, and to preserve dying industries would require the stifling of new. A degree of stability can be achieved under a Communist system but only at fearful cost.

Considerable progress has been made in the past generation toward lessening the severity of business fluctuations. Much of this has been due to structural changes within the economy, including more internal financing of business investment, more long-range business planning, changes in the banking system, control of stock markets, and more flexible Federal Reserve policies. The severity of fluctuations has also been lessened by the phenomenal growth of employee retirement plans and the introduction of unemployment insurance and social security. Structural and political changes such as these have made for increased stability without impairing the dynamic character of the economy. With this greater stability we are likely to have fewer severe economic emergencies, and with the understanding we now have of the economy, we are in a far more effective position to deal with those that may arise. Nevertheless, a measure of instability will always be with us.

If instability is part of the cost of a free economy, it is as much in the interests of business as in the interests of labor that that cost be broadly shared and not permitted to fall too heavily on the segment of the population least able to bear it. This is not merely a matter of ethics and morality but of realism. Unemployment compensation and social security serve an essential economic purpose in helping maintain purchasing power; they serve an essential political purpose in helping maintain confidence in the business system.

Similarly, the prohibition of monopolies and restraints of trade and the policing of trade practices not only protect the business system against undermining from within but greatly enhance confidence that economic power is not being used for unscruplous purposes. Regulatory commissions such as the Interstate Commerce Commission, the Federal Power Commission, the Federal Communications Commission, and the various state public service commissions have been great bulwarks against the nationalization of public utilities. These agencies are often a source of annoyance to the management of the utilities, and may at times be unduly restrictive in their regulatory policies, but they are a necessary condition for the preservation of at least a modified form of private enterprise in industries which elsewhere have been taken over entirely by government.

Because of the necessity for broad political support, our kind of system is strengthened by correcting extreme disparities in income, as through the progressive income tax and inheritance taxes. The businessman may feel that the actual rates imposed are unnecessarily punitive, that they severely restrict incentives for economic growth, and that the broad interests of society would be better served by a degree of moderation; nevertheless, he recognizes that the status of business is more secure if the extremes between great wealth and abject poverty are kept within reasonable bounds.

A strong trade union movement also tends to strengthen the business system by increasing public confidence in its over-all justice, by assuring workers that they do not stand alone and unprotected, and by showing there are powerful forces in the society which are explicitly dedicated to the welfare of workers. It is inconceivable that our present economic system with its vast numbers of workers and relatively few businessmen could exist for long without a strong and independent labor movement. This does not argue for the unionization of all workers; the needs of the economy and the interests of workers themselves are best served by a "mixed" system. Organized labor should be strong enough to protect its members and to keep all managements, unorganized and organized alike, alert to the needs of their employees. But total or even substantial unionization of all workers would result in such an overwhelming concentration of economic power as to represent a serious threat to the institutions of a free society. The interests of workers—all workers—as well as society are best served by a labor movement that is strong enough to be a significant force but not so strong that it can impose its will without let or hindrance, or in the security of its strength neglect the concerns of its members.

The emergence of a strong labor movement, with power already greater in some respects than would ever be permitted business, has created serious problems of its own. These are not relevant, however, to the present discussion, which is simply to note that one consequence of the labor movement has been to help reassure workers and the public that the economic power of business will not be used for narrowly selfish purposes. In the context of a discussion of liberalism and conservatism, it is perhaps worth noting also that in many respects the labor movement is an essentially conservative force concerned with resisting changes initiated by business.

There is need for business to join in the support of policies that will contribute to the long-range health of the society as a condition for the long-range security and opportunity of business. A case in point is the status of the Negro. While Negroes have made remarkable progress in this country during the last hundred years, they are still not full participants in the good things of American life and this lag represents a hazard to business. The hazard is not merely the lower and more uncertain per capita purchasing power of the Negro market; of greater moment is the underutilization of the human resources of the Negro population, arising in part from lack of adequate educational opportunities but more importantly from lack of sufficient incentive for the Negro to make the most of his capacities.

A more subtle but far more dangerous consequence of racial discrimination is the schism it creates in the body politic. A proletariat—which Toynbee defines as a group that is "in" but not "of" the society—is always a threat to social stability. The only group that fits this description in America today is the Negro, and he fits it only too well. If we continue to refuse the Negro full participation because of his color, and thereby continue to emphasize his color, we must not be surprised, as he gains political strength, to find him behaving first as a

Negro and only secondarily as a full-fledged citizen. If he is denied the white man's opportunities he may seek to take some of the white man's power away from him. This he might well be able to do considering the high concentration of the Negro vote and its susceptibility, through heightened race consciousness, to demagogic appeals and boss control.

Business has a stake in helping avoid such a schism. In a real sense, only business is in a position to deal positively with some of the underlying forces. There are many aspects to the problem: education, housing, acculturation, prejudice in all its forms and manifestations. The economic aspect, however, is fundamental, and this the businessman can do something about by providing more nearly equal economic opportunity on a basis of individual merit without regard to race.

An industrial economy provides a better atmosphere for working out the problems of relations between the races than a nonindustrial. This is clearly seen, for example, in the handling of school integration problems in the South. It is significant that where business groups are powerful, as in North Carolina and Florida, businessmen tend to caution moderation on the part of political leaders and to keep in check some of the more rabid forms of racial demagoguery. Because industry needs stability, new southern industries tend to locate in areas where there is the best promise of avoiding severe racial tensions. In both the South and the North it is likely that in the long run industry will provide the framework within which can be worked out some reasonably satisfactory solutions for the most intractable single problem of American society, the relations between the races.

III

Unfortunately, business has too often allowed other groups to assume the initiative in areas of economic and social policy.

And because businessmen have been opposed to many of the specific proposals advanced in the name of liberalism, they have been forced into a position of pseudo-conservatism that seriously distorts their true role. Moreover, by resisting programs advanced under the guise of promoting the public welfare, business has permitted itself to appear as opposing the public welfare for the sake of its own self-interest. The resulting image has hardly narrowed the gulf between business and the public or strengthened the leadership of business on social issues.

The argument of the businessman with those who seek to further courses of action to which he is opposed is not an argument between conservatism and liberalism; neither is it a question of acting or not acting in the face of urgent social problems. Properly conceived, the argument is simply one of method. If the businessman has a realistic grasp of the place of business in society he cannot be blind to the need for action on many fronts: to preserve public confidence in the business system, to mediate the stresses and strains of a dynamic economy, to facilitate the processes of innovation. The businessman, however—if he has not been too bady misled by his assumed conservatism with its implied commitment to the status quo—has his own ideas about the kind of action that ought to be taken.

Those who wear the mantle of liberalism are likely to think primarily in terms of government action when dealing with problems requiring attention. Businessmen, on the contrary, are likely to show a strong preference for voluntary forms of action. The so-called liberal often seems to care little for costs, in contrast to the businessman who has been trained in a discipline where outgo cannot long exceed income. Such a liberal tends to think primarily in terms of ends without too much regard for means, whereas the businessman recognizes the need for carefully fashioning means to ends; the one looks toward final results, the other toward balancing costs and benefits. The so-called liberal is likely to seek quick, easy solutions—"pass a law"—that may grossly oversimplify or miss the real heart of the problem and perhaps create serious complications of its own. The businessman is more likely to be concerned with the concrete reality of problems and their complexities and to have greater faith in the potentialities of people and of free institutions to work out effective solutions without undue outside intervention.

In this struggle the businessman finds himself at a disadvantage. If he opposes a massive public works program to alleviate unemployment, he is charged with lack of concern for the unemployed. If he opposes a mammoth public housing program because of its cost, he is charged with being more interested in money than in people. If he urges that economic adjustments be allowed to work themselves out through free market processes, he is charged with having no policy except a policy of drift. If he opposes high and rigid price supports for agriculture, he is charged with callous unconcern for the plight of the farmer. If he expresses anxiety over the growing power of organized labor, he is accused of wanting to destroy the labor movement. If he argues for methods and rates of taxation that will be less punitive to business and more favorable to economic growth, he is charged with greed for profits—a charge that carries greater weight because of his own professed commitment to self-interest as the rationale of business life.

Businessmen must find ways of presenting the courses of action they espouse in a manner that will communicate their concern for human values and not merely the interests of business. This will require greater initiative in putting forth proposals rather than simply reacting to the proposals of others. It means greater alertness to emerging social and economic needs, and willingness to act before the pressure of events forces action or before the situation develops to a point where demands for drastic and far-reaching action command wide public support. It also means willingness to consider concrete measures, for these are easiest for the public to grasp and understand. Business must be concerned with the forms of its programs and not merely their substance, because form largely determines communicability.

What needs to be communicated is not only the technical nature of the problem at hand and its proposed solution but above all the attitude of concern of those doing the proposing. Within a company the effectiveness of employee relations policies depends not only on what they are but on what they mean in terms of management's attitudes toward those in its employ. So too in the larger field of social policy. Business needs to promote a better understanding of the lines of action it supports, but it needs also to demonstrate—not by words alone but by the nature of the action itself—its concern for human welfare.

This may call for legislation in specific cases, and the businessman must learn to overcome some of his traditional distrust of government per se. If nongovernmental solutions are available there is great advantage in using them, and much of the businessman's effort should be directed toward finding or developing such solutions and applying them with vigor and effectiveness. There are circumstances, however, under which recourse to government is unavoidable or simply the most efficient method of procedure.

The real question is the manner in which government acts. For example, with respect to such pressing current problems as the maintenance of high levels of employment, the restoration of agricultural prosperity, the preservation of industrial peace, and the provision of more adequate health and medical services, the great question of public policy is whether to attempt to set things right by direct governmental fiat or to utilize government as a means for aiding in the creation of optimum conditions in which a free citizenry can deal with the problems themselves.

In the field of economic policy the need is to strengthen the ability of private enterprise to perform its economic functions. Too often the effort has been made to find some kind of substitute, usually in the form of government intervention. Too often, also, in the pursuit of aims that in themselves may be good, an inadvertent consequence may be the further shackling of private enterprise, thus requiring still further intervention by government. While it is important to provide reasonable protection for the unemployed, it is even more important to promote policies that will facilitate the absorption of the unemployed through vigorous economic growth. This may require action in areas with little obvious relation to unemployment as such: for example, modification of the tax laws to encourage capital formation. It is ironic to see policies put forward in the name of liberalism which would further impede the financing of the huge capital investments required to maintain a constantly higher standard of living and to provide employment for an increasingly large work force. It would be much more realistic—and much more in keeping with any meaningful concept of liberalism—to seek means for capitalizing on the dynamics of free economic institutions.

The so-called liberal often fails to examine what people need in the light of what they can afford. Unquestionably there are great needs for slum clearance and low-income housing; unquestionably too, the magnitude of these needs is such that some degree of government assistance is necessary. But the amount and kind of government assistance is another matter. If the government should go deeper in debt to finance a mammoth urban renewal and housing program—which might very well be "needed"—it is likely to create more inflation and bring on still greater problems of slums and housing, and a host of other problems as well.

The businessman's quarrel with the so-called liberal is that his propensity for certain types of government action undermines rather than strengthens group and individual self-sufficiency, encourages dependence on authority, and makes recourse to government increasingly necessary in dealing with future problems. He sees in this approach much of the same basic lack of confidence in people, much of the same distrust of spontaneity and obsession with centralization and control fostered in industry by the worst features of scientific management. He is disturbed at the tendency toward paternalism pursued by persons he suspects of being more the patrons than the compatriots of those they profess to serve, more interested in the aggrandizement of their own status and power than in the welfare of those for whom they claim to speak.

IV

Somehow or other the labels "liberal" and "conservative" have gotten mixed up. To change the metaphor, the cloak of conservatism fits the businessman as poorly as the cloak of liberalism fits many who profess that faith—as though someone had made a mistake in the check room.

The confusion in terms traces back to an initial confusion about the nature of liberalism. The concept of liberalism embraces two fundamental ideas: the idea of freedom and the idea of concern for human welfare. The idea of freedom has been taken over by business and the idea of human welfare by groups who are often critical of business. This division was fostered by the ideology of self-interest, which made it difficult for business to admit concern for human welfare even when its actual practice expressed substantial concern. The businessman thus shied away from the label of liberalism because it had been appropriated by others with whom he was often in disagreement and applied to social policies to which he was often strongly opposed. If he was not a liberal with the meanings that term had begun to acquire, then he must be a conservative, and so he has tried to be, with considerable confusion to all.

But the ideas of freedom and of concern for human welfare cannot be separated with impunity. Neither is complete without the other, and the effort to promote either at the expense of the other results in distortion and monstrosity. The businessman has a commitment to freedom but he must also be concerned for human welfare. The social reformer has a commitment to human welfare but in pursuing it he cannot afford to sacrifice human freedom, although in practice he often seems to do so simply because political measures, which are usually the only measures open to him, by their very nature involve elements of coercion and dependency.

On all counts liberalism is a more suitable philosophy for business than is conservatism. It fits the businessman's innovating role and emphasizes, as conservatism does not, the need for promoting social policies that will preserve and strengthen that role. The humanitarian aspect of liberalism underscores—again, as conservatism does not—the need for constant concern for the human impact of business actions and the obligation of business to serve the long-range public interest. The liberal viewpoint is more likely to encourage the exercise of initiative in recognizing and dealing with problems than is the conservatve. Liberalism implies a much stronger faith in the capacities of men and women than does conservatism with its more skeptical bias, and this, too, conforms more closely with the outlook of many businessmen. Not least important, the philosophy of liberalism provides a much more useful framework within which to relate business to the rest of society and to maintain confidence in the integrity and basic good will of business leadership.

V

If the businessman is going to be a liberal, he ought to be a thoroughgoing liberal. If he champions free enterprise, he ought equally to champion freedom in ideas, education, speech, and publication. He cannot afford to support freedom in economic affairs and demand conformity in others.

This means among other things that he must be tolerant of points of view other than his own, recognizing that no group has a monopoly on wisdom and that no group fully reflects the interests of all others, however much there may be of fundamental mutuality. Like the essence of the American economic system, the essence of democratic processes is the free interplay of ideas and the integration of varying interests into productive action.

Democracy is a rigorous and demanding form of social organization, as a free market is a rigorous and demanding form of economic organization. Democratic processes and free market processes are seldom neat and orderly; both create feelings of irritation or discomfort among those who like things systematic and predictable. A free economy no less than democracy requires a willingness to let people muddle through, make mistakes, in the faith that someway, somehow, everything will come out right. Essentially, a free economy requires—as democracy in fact means—a deep faith in people and in the inherent capacity of ordinary men and women to find a means for meeting and dealing with the problems they encounter.

For a democratic system to work, it must be kept in constant jeopardy. To live democratically is to live dangerously. So too with the economic system. If we set up too many safeguards, if we take too many precautions, we undermine the foundations of both systems. We can preserve democracy, as we can preserve free economic institutions, only by holding them in continuous danger of being destroyed from within— not by their enemies but by their friends, their own citizens who have freedom to act but who must be depended upon to act with judgment and restraint and with proper consideration for the general welfare as well as their own.

Essential to democracy is the idea of alternatives and freedom to choose between them. Freedom includes freedom to make a wrong or fatal choice. But it also includes freedom to make perhaps a better choice than has even been made before. Freedom is risky. Democracy is risky. A free economy is risky. But so is mankind. The social life of the ant is much safer than that of man, but that safety is secured at the sacrifice of further growth and development.

Democracy is a process, not a conclusion. Whether in industry or the larger reaches of society, the democratic way is nearly always the hard way. But compared with the authoritarian way, it is only harder in the short run. In the long run it produces better results with fewer complications. Above all it preserves alternatives for dealing with future problems, whereas the implications and consequences of an authoritarian solution severely limit the range of choice for dealing with situations that may arise out of the present one.

These are not matters of abstruse social philosophy; they are highly practical considerations of deep significance to citizens in all walks of life. Thoughtful businessmen will recognize and accept their special responsibility for helping strengthen these essentials of a free society—not simply because it is good for business but because they themselves are free men.

Index

Set in Times Roman
Format by Seamus Byrne
Manufactured by The Haddon Craftsmen, Inc.
Published by HARPER & BROTHERS, *New York*